SWEETWATER SAILORS

Great Lakes Merchant Marine:
The ships, the jobs, the men and women,
and their families

BOB OJALA
with Mike Braybrook

Sweetwater Sailors: Great Lakes Merchant Marine: The ships, the jobs, the men and women, and their families

ISBN: 978-1-734569-34-6

Library of Congress Control Number: 2020920635

Cover Design: Meredith Hancock, hancockmedia.com

Interior Layout & Formatting: Ronda Taylor, heartworkcreative.com

Published by The Unapologetic Voice House
Scottsdale, Arizona
www.theunapologeticvoicehouse.com

Dedication

To my father, Matt Ojala, who sailed the Great Lakes for thirty-two years.

I owe a large debt of gratitude to some experienced Great Lakes sailors, who contributed stories and photographs for this book. In particular, Mike Braybrook offered much time and wrote many working drafts of the stories contained herein. I worked aboard these ships, but did not have much actual sailing experience, so, with the help of these men and women, this book has become a true representation of what life was like aboard the ships, ferries, passenger liners, and tugs that operate on the Great Lakes.

Philip R. Clarke entering Duluth Harbor. *Photo Courtesy of Terry White.*

Railroad bridge at Grassy Island, Duluth, MN. *Photo Courtesy of Glenn Blaszkiewocz.*

Contents

Acknowledgments

First, to Mike Braybrook, who wrote many of the stories, offered his library of photos from his forty years of sailing, and edited my drafts, finding corrections and great improvements for this book. He was most knowledgeable and great fun to work with!

Next, in chronological order of receipt, I received stories and data from Chuck Cart, Bill Kulka, Captain Ed Wiltse, Randy Wilke, Captain Lori Renee Reinhart, Captain Stormi Sutter, Katrina Walheim, Sue Lieblein, Captain Aaron Menough, Joyce Greenisen-Estelle, and others. I hope they are all happy with the results. Many thanks to all of you!

Introduction

This is *not* a book about all merchant mariners. There are big differences in the lives and careers of deep-sea sailors and Great Lakes sailors. I respect them both. Both do a tough job, a job that the average person does not understand, and that outsiders think is somewhere between adventurous and romantic. Many people dream as children about sailing the seven seas. But if they knew how tough the Merchant Marine life can be, many would change their minds.

This book may occasionally refer to deep-sea and blue-water sailors and ships because they occasionally mix with the Great Lakes stories, but there have been many stories told and books written about the oceans and those sailors. The Great Lakes stories have been generally limited to their disasters, such as the *Edmund Fitzgerald*, the *Daniel J. Morrell*, the *Carl D. Bradley*, the Armistice Day storm of 1940, and so on. This book may mention those disasters because they effected the sailors' lives, but the main purpose of this book is to describe the lives of the Great Lakes sailors, including their work, the effects of their job on family life, and why they just couldn't quit.

I did not sail as a commercial merchant mariner. So, why am I writing this book?

My father was a Great Lakes merchant mariner, sailing from 1937 until 1970. His career effected our family. All of my early life was effected by his sailing, in both good and bad ways. But it did lead to my career focusing on the maritime industry. My father started taking 8mm movies back in the 1950s, showing the building of the Mackinac Bridge, Coast Guard icebreakers, loading and unloading ports, and accidents on the Great Lakes. However, this book is not meant to be a biography of my father's career. It will only be referenced as an example, where needed.

Many pictures are included in this book and can be found at the end of each chapter. Unless specifically mentioned, most photos were from my collection or my father's.[1,2] Many captains and sailors, including Mike Braybrook[3] and Captain Lori Reinhart, as well as other sailors who sailed on ore carriers and car ferries, have submitted photos that were used in this book.

I joined the Coast Guard because of those early memories, serving on two Great Lakes icebreakers, then went to college to become a naval architect, and spent a long employment with the American Bureau of Shipping (ABS), working as a field surveyor. Although I was on the Great Lakes for seventeen years, I inspected both Great Lakes and ocean freighters. This led me to start a marine consulting business, surveying—aka inspecting—ships. In my business, I worked on ships and in shipyards around the world.

It would not have been right for me alone to describe the life of these sailors, and particularly not on the numerous Great Lakes car ferries. Therefore, I enlisted the help of Mike Braybrook, who sailed for forty years, thirty-six of which were on the Great Lakes. There was also major input received from several chief engineers: Katrina Walheim, Joyce Greenison-Estelle, Chuck Cart, and Bill Kulka, who provided stories and ship details of the Great Lakes maritime industry. Several ship captain's stories are included in this book, particularly Lori Reinhart, who is currently the only female U.S. flag cargo ship captain on the Great Lakes. We needed to keep some balance between the "forward-enders" and "aft-enders."

Until around 1970, it was unusual to see women on these ships, except as cooks and stewards.[4] On the car ferries, women were room stewardesses and worked in food service for the passengers. Possibly because of the Vietnam War, the shortage of officers in the marine crews brought women into the roles of mates and engineers. More will be included on women's roles as the book progresses.

The car ferries on the Great Lakes were originally owned and operated by the railroads. Most of the employees were railroad employees. Their work schedules and job descriptions varied from those sailors on the Great Lakes cargo ships, so the car ferry sailors will be addressed as well, to show those differences.

As an ABS surveyor and as an independent marine surveyor who has conducted numerous surveys, I have had a good deal of contact with tug and barge operators on the Great Lakes. The activities of the tugboaters varied between each port on the Great Lakes, but each of these operators was colorful in their own way. There is one chapter in this book devoted to the Great Lakes tugboat industry. Randy Wilke assisted with some of those stories about tugboat sailors.

BOB'S INSPIRATION FOR THIS BOOK

My father, Matt Ojala, was a typical Great Lakes sailor of the early to mid-twentieth century. His story was the original inspiration for this book. However, it seemed like the book should cover all Great Lakes sailors, not just one, and this is the result.

I know my father had minimal formal education, although he eventually became quite well self-educated, being able to study marine engineering sufficiently to pass several U.S. Coast Guard licensing exams. My dad told me he only had a third-grade education, and I always thought he was joking. We found out later he remained in school until he was about thirteen years old, repeating grades due to his poor English. His lack of formal education kept him constantly on my back to continue my education in college. When I decided to join the U.S. Coast Guard instead of going directly to college at the age of 17, my father was very unhappy. However, he was thrilled when I later decided to attend college, after my four years in the Coast Guard.

My father told me he had gone to work at a paper mill in Cloquet, Minnesota, near Duluth, when he was a young teenager. When the

Depression hit, he went sailing. I never heard details about him finding a career as a sailor, but I assume he met a local Duluth-area man who was already a sailor. Because the money was very attractive during the Depression, and shore jobs were scarce, Dad went sailing in July 1937. He was just twenty-seven at the time, and he told me he had intended to quit sailing after the Depression but the ships "got into his blood." I still have my father's original discharge book, showing every ship he sailed, with sign-on and sign-off dates. That book shows the downside of the profession, showing ten and a half to eleven months' sailing time each year, with no vacations in those days. One year, he sailed right through the winter, being gone nearly twenty-three months between visits home.

Many of my early childhood memories were from trips to meet my father at various ports on the Great Lakes. I remember riding on my father's back, hanging onto his neck, as he carried me up the ladder onto his ship until I was old enough to climb the ladder myself. The other crew members enjoyed our visits, and we went home wired from all the soda, candy, and bakery sweets the crew fed us during our visits. Names like Captain Rapp and Chief Dugan became part of the family vocabulary.

We would occasionally travel long distances for these visits to see my dad, taking car ferries from Menominee, Michigan (across the river from Marinette), or Kewaunee, Wisconsin. The ferries crossed Lake Michigan to places like Ludington or Muskegon, Michigan. I remember swimming in Lake Michigan for the first time on one of those visits and wondering why people wanted to swim in such cold water because our beaches on shallow Green Bay were so warm.

We also drove up to Port Inland, Michigan, near Marquette, several times, where we would wait on a dark, deserted loading dock for hours. Those waits always seemed to be at night, and the boats always seemed to be late. Our trips to meet Dad's boat in Milwaukee were always a treat because we stayed with my uncle Adrian (Ade) Dupuis and his family on those trips. Uncle Ade always enjoyed visiting with my dad, so it made the trips more interesting. Trips to visit my father onboard the boats continued to define my life during my Coast Guard years, when I met my dad in Detroit and Green Bay while I was stationed in those port cities. These events also continued after my marriage, when my wife and I picked up my father from his last ship, upon his retirement at the Port of Toledo, Ohio, while I was a student at the University of Michigan.

As a Great Lakes sailor before the new union vacation plan, my dad was unable to take time off during the sailing season. He missed every birthday, my sister's wedding and my wedding, all of our graduations, and other special events if they occurred between March and the next January. That included Christmas! Because Dad was rarely home for Christmas, we saved some of our gifts to have a "second Christmas" when Dad came home. This constant stress on family life finally led to the divorce of my parents in 1959.

My father died in 1978, at the young age of sixty-eight. My dad always said he hated sailing, yet he became bored quickly after a few weeks at home. He never acquired any hobbies to look forward to when he came home each winter. This followed through to retirement, and his lack of activity quickly destroyed his health, resulting in heart failure. Take this as a good lesson—develop enough hobbies and activities to keep both mind and body alive and healthy, before and after retirement.

My father was well liked and respected by his fellow crew members, and although he was seldom home, his work ethic carried over into my life. He didn't have to be home to be a good role model.

HISTORICAL RECORD

Although this book was not originally intended to be a history of these Great Lakes merchant mariners, or the ships themselves, we started finding great stories and photographs from both old and new ships, and also noted the changes in the various job descriptions over the years. Ships on the Great Lakes often reach one hundred years and the ships themselves became part of our Sweetwater Sailors story. The old ships are still with us today, some still sailing, others as floating museums.

For this reason, you will find subsections in each chapter of the book: lake freighters, car ferries, tugboats, and passenger liners, even bumboats. These subsections deal with *the old and the new*, which will point out the physical changes and differences of the vessels over the last hundred years and more. Plus, the changes in designs over those years will be described. There are differences in the jobs, particularly between the old steamboats and the new diesel propulsion systems, but union contracts have also combined and eliminated some jobs. Some job differences vary between shipping lines; these changes will be described as much as possible.

There have been numerous books written about the shipping companies and the ship designs on the Great Lakes, and wherever possible, references will be made to those books.

This book is not meant to be a complete history of the Great Lakes or its sailors, but exists to honor these dedicated men and women who spend a huge percentage of their lives aboard ships and away from their families. If this book entertains the readers enough to catch their attention, I hope those readers will locate some of the referenced books and learn more about the history of this vital part of the American industrial economy. The chapter on boat nerds near the end of this book provides further sources of such information.

Canadian merchant mariners have similar stories to tell, but I had no Canadian collaborators for this book and, therefore, had no specific details of contracts and history. I did not intend to slight Canadian sailors, but maybe that could be the start of another book.

HISTORY OF WOMEN SAILORS ON THE GREAT LAKES

When this book was just an idea, it was going to be based on my father's career as a Great Lakes merchant mariner. In those days there were no women on Great Lakes cargo ships, other than the wives of the senior officers who occasionally sailed as passengers for a few weeks. Passenger ferries and passenger liners had women in the crew, but none in the deck or engine departments.

When I started working on ships as a marine surveyor, back in 1974, the only women in the crew were a few cooks and stewards, and most of them were married to the other cook on board. However, during the Vietnam War, there was a shortage of sailors (and officers in particular) on the Great Lakes. Sailors were drafted or they took better-paying jobs on deep-sea freighters going to Southeast Asia.

Partly to address this shortage of officers, the Great Lakes Maritime Academy (GLMA) was established in 1969. Based in Traverse City, Michigan, it is associated with Northwestern Michigan College (NMC). GLMA was kind enough to send me their *50th Anniversary Book* and has allowed me to use their book's information in this book.

I had originally asked GLMA to provide some history of women who attended GLMA, and they said there was a short chapter dedicated to that subject in their book. I was impressed by the honesty of GLMA in the following quotes:

> "The academy was established in 1969 as a maritime college to train men and women to be licensed mariners on ships of unlimited tonnage or horsepower …"

The book also states that between 1972 and 1974, the NMC Course Catalog included the following qualification for admittance:

> "Each applicant must: 1) be a male citizen of the United States."

The first woman enrolled at GLMA in 1976 and dropped out a year later. But as she dropped out, there were already four more women enrolled, and by March of 1979, there were six women enrolled in the program, five as deck officers, and one as an engineer. In 1979, a woman on the NMC board of directors stated the GLMA needed to begin to actively recruit "well-qualified women."

Finally, in 1980, the first woman graduated from GLMA as a deck officer. In the same year, eleven new women cadets enrolled for the fall semester, and the director of admissions stated, "The Academy now has the highest percentage of women enrolled in any (maritime) academy in the U.S." Those women were part of "eighty-one new students selected from a pool of 793 applicants, chosen based on ACT scores, references, work experience, general accomplishments in high school and other similar criteria."

The hard work of these "women pathfinders"—the GLMA's words—started to pay off and they began to graduate. About 10 percent of cadets have been female since 1982. Many of those cadets have earned awards like Maritime Cadet of the Year, Deck Cadet of the Year, and Engine Cadet of the Year.

The GLMA women have been active in such organizations as Women's International Shipping and Trading Association (WISTA) and Women on the Water (WoW). The GLMA women cadets hosted the first annual WoW Conference on the GLMA campus in 2006, and they hosted another WoW Conference in 2017, when over 150 guests attended, representing all five of the State Maritime Academies, the U.S. Merchant Marine Academy, and an Ontario Academy.

SUCCESS OF WOMEN MERCHANT MARINERS

Although GLMA has done a good job to prepare women for their professional roles as Merchant Marine officers, the women who graduated from GLMA, as well as the "hawsepipers," did not find it easy to get jobs, or to get promoted once they were hired as junior officers. Although I was unable to get factual information from GLMA, other sources show that as of today, there is only one woman who has made it to captain on a U.S. flag Great Lakes freighter. There are some female captains in the Canadian fleet.

Per Wikipedia, hawsepiper is an informal maritime industry term used to refer to a merchant ship's officer who began his or her career as an unlicensed merchant seaman and did not attend a traditional maritime college/academy to earn the officer license.

There are many female mates and engineers. Some earned the rank of chief engineer, and they are well respected by the crews.

Most sailors judge their workmates, even their officer supervisors, by whether or not they know their job, and how well they perform. They might give a new woman a hard time for a while, maybe even joke about women not being able to do their job. But, hopefully, the Academy prepared them for such ribbing, because it happens to all new sailors, including new male officers as well.

The hawsepipers—both men and women—who reach the officer level totally through hands-on experience, from deckhand up to mate, or from wiper/oiler up to engineer, get the respect of the crew much faster. Those men and women did all the physical labor alongside the rest of their crewmates from the start. However, hawsepiper women have an even tougher time getting promoted because company management assumes they don't have the necessary credentials or experience to be a good senior officer.

Until recent years, part of the discrimination can be laid upon the managers in the shipping company offices. They are responsible for choosing the crew and recommending people for promotions. They were generally older captains and chief engineers. Those men were typically hawsepipers themselves and were promoted from a sailing job to a job in the office as a manager. They were judging new prospective officers against their own experience, and part of that experience is being a man, working in what they believe is a man's world. That attitude is changing with college graduates coming in as new managers. Although those attitudes changed more quickly in other professions, it took longer to change in the Merchant Marine.

Women were historically considered a bad omen if they were allowed to sail aboard a ship, even as passengers. The sailors of the eighteenth and nineteenth centuries were very superstitious. If a woman was aboard a ship that sank or was suspected of falling off the edge of the "flat earth," thus never to return, it was probably assumed the woman's presence had something to do with the disaster.

Hopefully, the twenty-first-century sailors know better, but until all of those twentieth-century managers (mostly ex-sailors) retire from their positions of authority in the shipping company offices, it can be assumed their chauvinistic attitudes will remain.

At least the crews who happen to have women officers on their ships have come to respect them. It still comes down to personalities. If the female officers can joke and play the word games their crewmates throw at them, they will gain respect and succeed. As you will see in the stories in the other chapters of this book, practical jokes, crazy escapades "up the street," and some rough language is commonplace on every ship. If these women can handle that and respond in kind, they will eventually be called a shipmate, just like their male counterparts.

Women should be given the chance to succeed in this previously all-man's world. However, they cannot expect the crew to stop swearing and start treating the women differently than the men in the crew. The women need to develop a thick skin and fit in.

Until recent years, the majority of the unlicensed crew came from a rough background, many without a high school diploma, so they were tough, and expected the other crew, including women, to be the same. Just like management, the crews today are better educated and more aware of women in the workplace. However, as one captain told me, he knew trouble would result if he saw one of the male crew members being overly polite to a female crew member. And if two men were treating her with unexpected respect, the two guys would eventually start fighting.

It is still the real world, and men and women will act like all human beings, even aboard ships.

1. Mackinac Bridge Construction

2. Mackinac Bridge Construction

3. Mike Braybrook, major contributor

4. Women were only cooks, prior to 1970.

CHAPTER ONE

Basic Differences Between Great Lakes and Deep-Sea Sailors

You will notice in the following descriptions and stories that the ore carriers on the Great Lakes, as well as the car ferries, are usually referred to as boats. Yes, we on the Great Lakes know all those definitions showing the difference between ships and boats, and you certainly cannot place any of these Great Lakes ships on a larger one, thus defining them small enough to be a boat. However, they are ore boats, even if 1000-feet long, and they are not called ore ships. They have been called boats for over a hundred years, and it is too late to change it! Most ships on the Lakes are called boats!

So, what are some of the basic differences between the deep-sea, or blue-water, sailors and their Great Lakes counterparts? The following may not be true in every case, but it will give you an idea of how the two sailors' careers do vary in many respects.

The Great Lakes are often referred to as "the Lakes" and the cargo ships as "Lakers," so you will occasionally see those references, particularly in the firsthand stories from the collaborators.

CONTRACTS

The major difference is the length of the contracts back in the "old days"—or most of the nineteenth and twentieth centuries, versus the much shorter contracts today. My father started sailing in 1937 and often started his contract in late winter, usually February or early March. The season ended the following winter, either December or early January. Deep-sea contracts varied in length, but because of their typically longer voyages, those contracts were generally one or more round trips to and from their home port. When the ship returned to that home port at the end of the contract, the sailor could sign another contract, or sign off, go home, and then sign on to another ship after some time at home. Because most of the Great Lakes ore boats—ships, if you prefer—stopped sailing during the worst of the winter months, the machinery was shut down and "laid up" before the engineers could leave the ship; that would normally take seven to fourteen days. The boilers were drained and the sea chests filled with grease, and all water pipes on the ship were drained and blown down with air. The following spring—if February is considered spring—the engineers returned to the ships for fit-out. Fit-out was the reversal of the lay-up procedure, and it usually involved getting a small donkey boiler going, and then filling and firing the main boilers, filling the domestic water lines, bleeding heating lines of air, et cetera, before the captain and deck crew returned. A donkey boiler is an extra small boiler onboard the ship. It is used to supply steam for heat and deck machinery, like winches, when the main boilers are shut down. The name derives from the tradition of using draft animals for the winch work before the invention of steam power.

Also, there was usually a long list of minor machinery repairs from the previous season, which needed to be completed before the ship sailed. I remember my father working two, even three weeks aboard before the deck crew returned. This was paid time, but it was not listed in their record as sailing time, and the same was true for the time laying up the ship. Sailing time began when the ship left the dock for the first voyage of the season and stopped when the ship was tied up at the end of the season. If the ship happened to be in dry dock over the winter, many of the engineers stayed during that extra time as well.

Once the sailing season began, the crew generally sailed the entire season, unless they were relieved for a serious illness. The longest time my father sailed—including fit-out and lay-up—was twenty-three months, from the time he left to fit out a ship in February until he returned two January's later. The reason for this extremely long contract was his ship sailed on a coal run for a power plant in Detroit, carrying coal from Toledo. Because the power plant needed coal year-round, his ship sailed through the ice on Lake Erie, with the help of Coast Guard icebreakers. My sister and I did not see him during that entire period. However, my mother did sail with him for a week each summer.

These days, sailors have contracts of sixty on, thirty off or even thirty on, thirty off, but in my father's days of sailing, which ended in 1970, he never had a vacation during the sailing season. He missed every Thanksgiving, every Easter. He only made it home for two Christmas holidays that I can remember. We always saved a few Christmas gifts to open when Dad came home! My father also missed every graduation and both my sister's and my weddings because he was told he could leave, but there was no guarantee he would have a job when he returned.

Each winter, my father complained about the terrible life he led and the storms he survived. My mother begged him to search for a shore job at the local paper mills, believing they needed boiler operators. But the money was certainly better as a sailor in those days, and after about ten days at home, my father would get bored and start staring at the phone, waiting for his call to go back to another ship.

My father was part of a dying breed of Scotch boiler mechanics. He probably could have used that expertise to demand some vacation time, because he knew they needed him. But Dad was loyal to his company and did not want to push his weight around. So he sailed for thirty-two years, never taking a vacation during the sailing season. He was proud of the fact that his last two ships, the *Ben W. Calvin* and the *United States Gypsum*—both with Scotch boilers—were scrapped within two years of his retirement. He said they couldn't run them without him, and that may have been partially the reason. The problem was, Dad sat idle after he retired, smoked too much (four packs a day), and died just seven years later. Sailors never had time to find hobbies or go fishing, so retirement was boring and a death sentence for them.

The Scotch marine boiler is a firetube boiler, in which hot flue gases pass through tubes set within a tank of water. The general layout is that of a squat horizontal cylinder. One or more large cylindrical furnaces are in the lower part of the boiler shell. Above this, there are a large number of small-diameter fire tubes. Gases and smoke from the furnace pass to the back of the boiler then return through the small tubes, moving up and out of the chimney. Scotch boilers are generally lower pressure and have "wet steam."

The Scotch boilers differ from the design of the larger high-pressure water tube boilers. In the latter, water circulates in tubes heated externally by the fire. Fuel burns inside the furnace, creating hot gas. The tubes (called steam-generating tubes) are typically embedded in the walls of the boiler. The bottom ends of the tubes are connected to a water drum, and the top end of the tubes are connected to a steam drum. Additional tubes are used as "superheaters," and remove all of the moisture. Some boilers have extra tubing in the stack, called economizers, to preheat water before it is fed into the water drum.

As mentioned earlier, the engineers usually had that two-week lay-up period after sailing stopped, and another two-week fit-out before sailing started, typically making the engineer's season one month longer than the "forward-enders," as the captain and mates were called.

SHORT RUNS

Another major difference between the Great Lakes and the blue-water sailors' lives is the Laker's short runs from one port to the next and the extremely short loading and unloading time for their bulk cargoes, particularly on the self-unloading bulk cargo ships on the Great Lakes. In the example given above, that coal run from

Toledo to Detroit was under twelve hours, then took six to eight hours to unload, and then the ship went back to Toledo for another load.

Blue-water ships, other than some coastal operators, sail from Europe to the Great Lakes, Europe to Baltimore, China to Los Angeles, and so on. Other than some occasional short runs, like the Caribbean routes, the voyages are three days, seven days, or even longer. Most of the ocean cargo in the early twentieth century was break bulk on pallets, finished steel products, and other items that required several days to unload. Modern container ships and car carriers can unload faster now, but their voyages are still longer than the short runs of just several days on the Great Lakes.

My mother would take us to meet my father's ship at various Great Lakes ports in Michigan and Wisconsin during the summer, where we might, at most, get six or eight hours at a loading port like Port Inland. Many times, that was in the middle of the night. The shame was, my Dad's ship was sometimes at anchor outside the harbor, and he could not always get to shore. One time, the deck crew knew his family was waiting for him on the dock, so they brought my Dad to shore in the ship's little skiff, to allow us more time together. If the weather was rough, they wouldn't take the risk to do that.

Once my father started sailing self-unloaders (the majority of the Boland & Cornelius fleet, which is now American Steamship), it was worthless to visit him at unloading ports because they would unload in five to six hours if all went well.

Because of the short runs between ports, seldom more than two or three days, even just ten to twelve hours on Lake Erie, and the very short time in port, the crew members who were not working (my father included) would run "up the street" for a quick shot and a beer. It was their only opportunity to be off the ship, and with the short stays in these ports, there was little time to do anything more. It's not that sailors around the world did not hit the bars, but there was no time for any other activity for Great Lakes sailors. Each Great Lakes port had bars just outside the steel mills, power plants, coal docks, and shipyards. In Chicago, there was Peckerhead Kate's near the shipyard, or the Golden Shell just outside the shipyard gate. There was also the Crow Bar, near the Calumet power station. Those were interesting places, with a lot of ladies getting free drinks from the sailors who frequented those bars.

There were similar bars in Green Bay, Gary, Duluth, Detroit, Toledo, Cleveland, Ashtabula, Buffalo, and Conneaut, and I spent time with my dad in some of them when I was in the Coast Guard. Then, once they got home, the sailors missed the conversations from those bar visits, and they spent too much time at bars around their homes, both with their family and without them, once they were bored with home life during the winter.

WEATHER

There are various weather differences between the Great Lakes and oceans. Many deep-sea sailors, particularly the tugboat captains taking jobs on the Great Lakes, teased Great Lakes guys about being "puddle sailors," "fair-weather sailors," and other similar jabs. After those tugboaters experienced a major Great Lakes storm, they changed their minds. Most deep-sea guys know differently, and much of that kidding is just friendly. The Great Lakes region does not have hurricanes, but the weather on the lakes can be affected by hurricanes in the Gulf and East Coasts. The nor'easters are the dreaded storms on the Great Lakes, and those storms are generally the cause of Great Lakes disasters, such as the sinking of the *Edmund Fitzgerald*, which most people have heard about.

However, bad weather on the Great Lakes tends to build quickly, and the period of the waves—in other words, the distance between them—is much less than on the ocean. Instead of the large, rolling swells of ocean waves, the Great Lakes waves beat on a ship, giving little time to ride over them or recover from a roll.

As a marine surveyor and four-year Coast Guardsman, I have ridden ships enough to experience bad weather in the North Sea, the Baltic, the North Atlantic, the Caribbean, the Gulf of Alaska, and the Great Lakes. I have been prone to seasickness my entire life, and I must admit I have been "under the weather" on each of those bodies of water. While in the Coast Guard, I experienced a forty-five-degree roll on Lake Michigan, in twenty-foot waves. In the Gulf of Alaska, I experienced forty-foot seas, and in the Caribbean experienced thirty-foot seas with fifty-knot winds.

I tell you this background to show what sailors put up with on all large bodies of water, and the Great Lakes is no exception, as shown in photos by Mike Braybrook, seen at the end of this chapter.[2]

The following story from Chuck Cart is from his personal experience while sailing on the Great Lakes cement carrier *Paul H. Townsend*, which should dispel the rumor that the Great Lakes are typically calm:

> The Townsend *was built in 1945 as a Maritime Commission C1-M-AV1, small shallow draft cargo vessel. It was originally named the* Coastal Delegate. *Her old logbooks were still aboard when I was there in 1987 and 1988. She was converted to a cement carrier in 1951 and lengthened during the winter of 1957–58. She was known to be a handy little ship but prone to rolling.*
>
> *We left Green Bay, Wisconsin, after discharging our cargo of cement, and headed up the Bay in ballast, on our way to Alpena, Michigan, for another load. We had some bad weather, and the captain left instructions with the mate that when we got up to the Door—also known as Death's Door, the passage between Green Bay and upper Lake Michigan—he would take another look at the weather and decide if we should continue out into the lake. We arrived at the Door very early in the morning, and the mate on watch decided the weather was looking good to him. So he took the ship out into the lake, where we promptly got our butt kicked. The captain woke when his TV landed on the deck next to his bunk. I heard later that he wasn't very impressed.*

The spare main engine head—the main engine is a slow speed, Nordberg TSM-216 diesel, and the heads for the twenty-two-inch bore cylinders are quite large—came adrift. It was sliding back and forth across the upper engine room, crashing into the steps of the electric parts locker on the port side, and back across into the lube oil storage tanks on the starboard. I was on watch, and the oiler and I were able to lasso it with the overhead hoist, by flipping the hook at the lifting eye as it went by, until we snagged it and could lash it back down.

At the top of the ladder from the shop to the engine room, there was a parts locker, a double-door cabinet full of drawers containing small parts like shaft keys, small pins, nuts, washers, and so on. This cabinet tore off the bulkhead, and when it hit the deck, the doors burst open, spilling all the small drawers and their parts. We shoveled the now well-mixed little parts into five-gallon pails and spent the rest of the season sorting them out.

The paint locker was trashed, as well, with several inches of paint sloshing around in a tie-dyed pattern on the floor of the locker. The captain made the mate come clean up the paint; it was quite gratifying to see the mate in rubber boots, ankle-deep in paint, scooping it up with a dustpan, and pouring it into a five-gallon pail. When I got off watch, I went to my cabin to find that the waves hitting the front of the aft house had been squirting in around the gasket of my porthole, and my bunk was soaked.

Also, check out Mike's story about his Thanksgiving dinner on the *Irvin L. Clymer*, a meal that ended up a total disaster due to bad weather.

SHIP HANDLING AND UNUSUAL WEATHER

In addition to the severe weather pictures at the end of the chapter*, Great Lakes captains are expected to navigate congested waterways in ice, and other unusual weather and traffic conditions. Those pictures and commentary were provided by Captain Lori Renee Reinhart, who has sailed on the Great Lakes as a mate and captain since 1995. Captains must navigate narrow, winding rivers and ice-choked harbors on almost a daily basis.

Ocean cargo ship captains seldom work in ice, unless they are servicing some Arctic Russian ports, and when they are in congested harbors and channels, they will invariably have a pilot aboard familiar with those waters. On the Great Lakes, the Academy cadets take their pilotage exam before graduation, and as mates they log their experience in these waters. By the time they become captain, they have been observed by a senior captain, who reports to the company when the mate is ready. Before the company will give them the responsibility for a multi-million-dollar ship, they must get firsthand experience maneuvering these routes.

The photo titled Iced in at Duluth Harbor, in the back of this chapter,[3] used with the permission of Paul Scinocca, shows an icy day in Duluth harbor, steaming in the cold, with other vessels nearby. Ship handling is tough enough in a congested waterway, but a ship tends to follow fractures in the ice, making navigation even harder, and sometimes dangerous. Ships have often been dragged aground due to flowing ice conditions. Each fall and spring, vessels become mired in slush ice on the St. Mary's River, and in the Rock Cut Channel, below the Soo Locks. The Coast Guard icebreakers cannot be everywhere at once, so the freighter captains have to slug it out alone unless they become hopelessly stuck in the ice.

The photo tilted Captain Lori shows Captain Reinhart dressed for near-Arctic conditions, ten degrees below zero (Fahrenheit), when she was backing into a harbor through bridges in frigid weather.[4] This operation required her constant attention from outdoors on the bridge wings; captains must always be on the bridge during such maneuvers, giving navigation orders.

I include photos at the end of the chapter to show several extremely narrow and winding channels that these Great Lakes masters must navigate. You should look up harbors on the internet, like Cleveland, to see the winding Cuyahoga River, also in Green Bay, Wisconsin, to see the numerous, narrow bridges, or the Calumet River in Chicago, which is busy with both freighters and numerous carefree pleasure boaters.

The photo at the end of this chapter titled Gary was taken by Captain Reinhart outside Gary, Indiana, with her vessel stuck in the ice, waiting for tug assistance.[5] Captain Reinhart also shared a photo taken from the bow of her vessel showing that it was stuck in heavy ice at the Straits of Mackinac, waiting for Coast Guard help.[7]

The next photo titled Green Bay Bridge was taken in Green Bay, Wisconsin, heading through a narrow bridge in an ice-choked river.[6]

Captain Reinhart was stuck in the ice just outside the harbor in Duluth, Minnesota as well.[8] Winter operations are tough on the Great Lakes, but the shipowners try to stretch the season for as long as possible, to keep the steel mills stocked with ore over the winter.

Even when the weather is not a problem, the tight channels present challenges to a ship's captain.[9] If it is not another ship in a narrow channel, it's a river bend.[10] And then finally, there is a wide river with bridge spans just wide enough to pass![11]

Can you imagine what it is like to park? A photo taken by David Schauer, shows a freighter docking at an iron-ore loading dock in Duluth-Superior Harbor. That maneuver is like parallel parking a car but with an ore carrier 767 feet long and seventy feet wide.[12]

But there are rewards for operating on the Great Lakes. The sunsets are breathtaking.[13] And the reflections on the lakes are beautiful.[14]

Captain Reinhart shared some more thoughts with me on this topic:

Most mate cadets have their pilotage before they sail as mates. Most companies will have senior captains watching mates and advising company management who should be "given a shot." The mate would have had enough time to write their exam for their Great Lakes Master's License. From that point, the company will have the new officer observed by senior captains, who will let them ship-handle under strict supervision. This process can be a month or can take years depending on the officer's experience and capabilities. If you pass muster, you are given your first relief job on one of the ships where you observed.

The first time you maneuver a vessel on your own, it is one of the scariest times sailing. Every time you maneuver is different when sailing these vessels. Every docking is different. You have to have situational awareness at all times. My company keeps an extra mate in the pilothouse with the captain while maneuvering. I have to say, this is the best policy ever. The mate can take phone calls, talk to the bridges, etc., so the captain can concentrate on ship handling.

As one of my mentors used to say, "Position ... Position ... Position: if your boat isn't in the right place, stop and get it there, or abort!"

The Great Lakes is a small community, and none of us wants to see another captain in trouble. We go across company lines to give each other advice on docks and ports, which one captain may know better than another. I never feel stupid asking advice from retired captains or current captains, who may know something that can help in safely docking a ship. We all still take notes, so we can look up drafts with water gauges for certain channels, and what current flow we feel comfortable with while turning a vessel in a river, and so on.

Some of the tight river photos from Captain Reinhart were taken in the Cuyahoga River, in Cleveland, Ohio.[15] Great Lakes captains will tell you, the Cuyahoga is not only narrow, but it has some bends in the river that seem impossible to navigate.

The following story from Captain Aaron Menough not only tells about navigating the Cuyahoga but also describes the river as seen from an airplane arriving in Cleveland. It is a long narrative but explains the extremely stressful times when a captain is faced with

11

pressure from his company's office to keep moving yet they have weather that does not allow the ship to move safely.

The nonstop rain and wind made everything seem even more miserable for the flight. Circling Cleveland, Ohio, at one thousand feet provided a sense of excitement, as my bird's-eye view of the double omega–shaped Cuyahoga River came into view. This vantage point allowed me to witness the entire river in less than the blink of an eye, a sight that takes me five hours to transit on an average ship day.

The West Third Street Bridge was fixed in its open position, and the NS2 railroad had a small passenger train transiting its elevated corroded rails. The Eagle Avenue bridge (called Eagle Street by most captains) continued to stand open after ten years, leading right up to a hairpin ninety-degree corner we call Collision Bend. It was all available with perfect clarity, like a model train set, complete with a smokestack, rust-stained brick buildings, and dilapidated shelters of the past industrial era.

I flew over the heart of the post-war steel industry. I could see my future out of the airplane window. I could see my ship at the dock. Torrential downpours forced and squeezed all the water of the Ohio Valley into this tiny bottleneck and out into Lake Erie. As a result, the farmer's clay runoff mixed into the river water, making a giant mud milkshake, which grabbed all the river debris and garbage as it flowed.

My hands started to sweat when the plane banked into a turn and I was granted a view of Lake Erie, looking past the break wall where the mouth of the river makes its exit. The next mile and a half of Lake Erie outside the break wall was discolored from that river runoff.

Entire trees went floating by, parts of broken boats and rotted life jackets, Styrofoam in the shapes of everything, and random car tires and bits and pieces of clothing discarded from the hillside hobo villages. It all ended up in this mighty urban soup resembling an oversized toilet of epic proportions that had just been flushed.

My job was to go up it. I was going to navigate a 630-foot ship up that twisted concrete corridor.

I checked the flow of the current on an hourly basis. After many phone calls, my peers collectively speculated the current would begin its decline in the next twelve hours. Too much current for this boat is 1.5 miles per hour. Anything over that and this ship is too underpowered to make any right-angle turns. That is every turn in the Cuyahoga River. The meter was showing 2.0 mph. It would begin its decline, show some signs of weakening, and then quickly return to 2.0 mph again.

I silently thought to myself, there is nothing to worry about. As long as it stays over 1.5 mph, my pressure-exerting office cannot say anything. Even they know that it's outside the capability box.

Usually, my people in charge ask me what time I will be getting to the dock. I do my best to answer, but this only buys me so much time before they start getting impatient. "Time is money, time is money, you're costing us a thousand dollars an hour."

I read between the lines. They hang up after the phone call.

The river continued its trek. The ship remained stationary.

Two more days passed. My carpet continued to thin with my pacing. Two days on the Great Lakes is a lifetime. I stared at the computer, trying to determine the exact moment the river would be manageable. I started to see a significant drop off, 1.8, 1.7, almost manageable. A puff of smoke went by in the distance as I peered through the window of the pilothouse. I recognized one of the tugs from Great Lakes Towing, taking care of some business. I'd known the man driving the little 1940s cast iron war tug since we went to school together.

I called him and asked, "Brad, what's that current look like to you? Can I make it?"

"Well, it's dropping off. Have you considered taking two tugs, one on the bow and one on the stern? We could probably get you up there," he said.

"That's what I was thinking about doing but wanted to talk to you first," I said.

"Well, two would be the safest thing to do if you're worried about it, and of course, we appreciate the business," he replied.

Brad is a great guy. A real veteran of the Cuyahoga River, and you knew you could always breathe easy whenever he was on the tow. He knew every inch of that river, how to get up and down it, and was always safe. You never had to tell him what to do.

My anxiety began to melt as I made the three-hour call for the tugboats. We called the Buffalo next, which was moored across from us. I spoke with the lady captain (it was Lori Reinhart), so she knew what I was going to do. Just a courtesy call I suppose. I've talked to her over the radio several times in the past, and she was helpful, but I had never met her in person. I couldn't help but notice a touch of discomfort in her voice. When she learned that I was going up, it may have accidentally turned the burner on her from her office.

"You're going up now?" she asked tensely.

"Yes, as soon as the tugs get here, which will be about 2200," I replied.

There was a long pause followed by, "Well, I guess I'll just follow you up then."

This is the worst position you can be in because it's hard to explain to your office how another boat beat you to a dock that you've been staring at for three days, especially since the boat that beat you has only half the equipment. The Buffalo *is a ship that is designed to transit the Cuyahoga River. It has a very narrow stern, a perfect view all around the pilothouse, and, most importantly, a stern thruster. When combined with a bow thruster, you have an extremely maneuverable ship, which can move swiftly. Depending on who is driving, the* Buffalo *can get up the Cuyahoga River in about three hours compared to my five.*

"I'll wait about an hour or so," she said.

"OK, that's fine with me," I said.

"This way, I won't be chasing you right up on your stern the whole way," she continued.

"OK, thanks, I appreciate that. If you need me, I'm working radio channel sixty-six," I said so that she knew how to call me.

The tugs worked their way out to the harbor. I let go of the lines and made my way to Cleveland's inner pier. We then made the tugs fast, as I watched what I hoped would be the last of the debris. I looked at my wheelsman and said, "Here goes nothing."

I put the ship in gear, and we worked our way under the Norfolk Southern #1 Railroad Bridge.

The first few turns were slow as we got started. As we came around Superior bend and got lined up for Center Street, any fear I had quickly abated, as I concentrated just on what I was doing. I would use the bow thruster as much as I could, then ask the tug to pull my bow around, right before it looked like we were going to stop turning, and smash into the hobo villages. If my stern started to go the same way I was turning, I would use the tug that was running free to try and put his nose up against my hull and pin the stern in place.

This went on for hours. First Center Street, then Columbus Street, around the concrete corner of the "Alfa" Knuckle, and its jagged can-opening edge, which has been there for God only knows how many years. Continuing, we slid under the Flats

Industrial Railroad Bridge, and back up to Collision Bend, making the 110-degree turn under Eagle Avenue.

Pressing forward, I could hear the tired old Great Lakes tug give everything it had, and on several occasions, Brad informed me that we would have to slow down to make sure we didn't overheat the engines. Slowing down from ten to eight miles per hour, we were now doing about one-half mile per hour when we went under the Norfolk Southern #2 Railroad Bridge. Before my stern was clear, I was forced to make the next turn, so as not to hit the steel sheet wall at Cuyahoga River Products, another one of our customers.

Managing to not hit anything so far, two hundred more yards up, and my bow would be poking out underneath the West Third Street Bridge. This is going better than I thought, I reflected in silence.

I looked at my watch; it was two in the morning. Fatigue started to take effect, forcing me to put my head down in my arms for just a few seconds. My mates continued to give me distances off every object that I might hit, as I heard them over the radio in the front window. It didn't matter, whether it was thirty feet or eight feet, they all sounded the same. I was emotionally at rock bottom, wondering how I got to this place and time and how it would ever end.

Suddenly, it occurred to me that I hadn't heard the Buffalo *on the radio since I left. I looked on the electronic chart for her, and she had not moved an inch. A small sense of elation and pride came over me, making me feel like I could do something that a better-equipped boat couldn't do. (It turned out, Captain Reinhart was on the way to the hospital that day.)*

This was the boost I needed. I could feel the blood begin to course back through my tired body.

"This challenge is almost over," I said to myself. And I let out a huge sigh.

"Well, Ken," I said to my wheelsman. "All we have to do is go through the old Jefferson Street abutment, slide through 'the Twins,' somehow get through the River Terminal Bridge, tie up without hitting anything, and we're there," I said.

Jefferson Street is no problem except that before you're even through, you have to start turning again to get through "the Twins." That is the nickname given to these short, stubby, little old railroad bridges that are side by side. One is still actively used, about once a year. As a result, they will not tear it down. The other twin is an old, broken-down river traffic bridge. Jagged steel corners are coming out of everywhere and its rotted wooden support pilings fall into the river. The Twins sit right on a small, roughly thirty-degree left-hand turn, and even after you are lined up and going through the little draw, you only have about fifteen feet on one side, and twenty feet on the other side, which in Cuyahoga River terms is the equivalent of a mile.

After successfully negotiating that one, I had about five minutes of an actual straight course line to follow. There are only two in the entire river. This provided me with another personal moment to put my head down and wish myself back to a memory when I sailed with Clipper, the cruise line.

"Why did I give up Bonaire to be here in the back of a steel mill in Cleveland, Ohio?" I said to myself.

I then refocused. This will all be over in less than an hour, I thought. I will be tied up, and then I can lie down for approximately three hours before doing it all over again but backward.

I continued pushing my way up. The tugs, now sounding more tired than we did, were on their last breath. All three of us managed to squeeze through the microscopic space in the River Terminal Bridge.

My wheelsman continued to indirectly pump the blood out of my heart by saying things like, "We ain't going to make it at this rate."

"Rob?" I yelled into the radio.

"Hello?" he said.

"How much damn further do we have to go to clear this crap bridge?"

"Ohhh, about, maybe, it looks like …" he wailed into the radio, trying my patience even more.

I waited to hear the crunch of the bridge as I knew the last distance given was twelve feet and closing.

"You need about twenty feet ahead and you should start making room," Rob finally said.

I couldn't get my stern away from the wall unless I continued to drive ahead but I had no room to drive ahead. All the time the current continued to push me sideways rendering the bow thruster almost useless.

After several seconds, I heard, "Seventy feet now and widening," from my lookout.

"Thank God! How much farther ahead do I have to go to clear this bridge?" I repeated for the millionth time that night.

"You're fifteen and widening now, about twenty more feet ahead and you'll be all clear," said Rob.

The boat slowly, gradually, painfully straightened itself out on the last hundred-yard stretch. I could see the dock and the iron ore pile that I would be unloading onto.

After backing and filling, which is how we maneuver the last few feet into a tight space, I tied the boat up as fast as I could. I knew I only had three hours of unloading time here, and this would be the only time that I had to take a nap.

We let go of the tugs quickly but only one of the tug crew could go home. One of them had to stay behind to tow us back out.

SEASONAL LAY-UP

The majority of Great Lakes freighters lay up during the heavily iced months of the year. The vessels try to sail as long as possible, particularly those carrying iron ore, to be sure the steel mills are stocked through the winter. There were some years in the 1960–1980 era when many of the newer, structurally sound Lake boats sailed all winter. The ice damage to the vessels, plus the wear and tear on the Soo Locks, made the program economically unsound. Some vessels sail all winter on the lower Lakes, but the Soo Locks are closed in mid-January until late March.

I included a photo that shows a typical winter lay-up at one of the several Great Lakes shipyards (this one in Sturgeon Bay). [16] However, many of the vessels lay-up at other ports, like Buffalo and Milwaukee, where there are no shipyards, but the port is secure from heavy winds.

There is a later section in this book covering maintenance, but there are numerous small jobs that must be completed before the engineers can leave the ship for the winter: water pumps and pipes will freeze and the heating systems must be winterized. Several photos in the book show some of the crew, carrying out those tasks at the end of the season. [17, 18]

1. Rough Great Lakes weather.

2. Weather can be dangerous on deck.

3. Ice at Duluth Harbor entrance.

4. Captain Lori Reinhart, dressed for sub-zero weather.

5. Iced in while entering Gary, Indiana, harbor.

6. Tight City bridge in Green Bay, Wisconsin

7. Iced in and foggy, at Straits of Mackinac.

8. Ice conditions can be beautiful.

9. Tight fit in Cuyahoga River.

10. One of the many Cuyahoga turns.

11. Very tight Railroad bridge in Green Bay.

12. Parallel parking a 730-foot ship at the ore docks.

13. Beautiful Great Lakes sunset.

24

14. Beautiful refection while loading at the ore docks.

15. M/V Republic in the Cuyahoga River, Cleveland.

16. Winter lay-up at Sturgeon Bay, Wisconsin.

25

17. Maintenance done at winter lay-up.

18. Mike Braybrook doing winter maintenance.

CHAPTER 2

Working Lives of
Great Lakes Sailors

The following explanation of the Great Lakes merchant ship crews, as compared to ocean crews, comes from Chuck Cart, who sailed both the deep sea and Great Lakes, aboard Great Lakes ore boats, cement carriers, tug/barge units, and the carferry *Badger*:

> *There are generally three "departments" aboard a typical U.S. merchant vessel: deck, engine, and galley. If passengers are frequently carried—on some cargo ships—or it is a Coast Guard certified passenger vessel, a department may be added to interact with them. All crew members are required to hold a U.S. Merchant Mariner Credential with the proper endorsements and licenses, as well as a medical certificate and an identity card—now a TWIC, or Transportation Worker Identification Credential—issued by the Department of Homeland Security—or "Homeland Hysteria," as I calls them.*
>
> *I have worked in the engine room of steam and motor vessels of both Great Lakes and ocean-going vessels, and generally, they have been manned similarly: with a captain who is overall in charge, a deck department with a first or chief mate, one second mate, and one third mate as licensed officers. Then there*

are three to six able-bodied seamen, sometimes a bos'n, and as many ordinary seamen as needed to handle cargo.

The engine room crew consists of a chief engineer; first, second, and third assistant engineers; and occasionally extra engineers if the workload or contract calls for it. Then there are a varying number of unlicensed personnel, most often three oilers or qualified member of the engine department (QMED), and sometimes one or two wipers. On the self-unloading bulk carriers, the conveyor man—and sometimes an assistant— would be considered part of the engine room crew, but the gatemen were part of the deck department. On tankers, the pumpman—or again, sometimes an assistant—was part of the engine room crew as well.

The operation of the "plant" is much the same as well, although on the Great Lakes the trips are shorter, so there is more loading/unloading time, and more maneuvering time in rivers and harbors. In my experience, ocean-wise maneuvering was more of a concern for both the deck and engine depart- ments, where on the Great Lakes, it is just part of the usual watch duties. Some of the ocean vessels use a "day working" or "lock up" engine room system where the engineering crew works during the day and one of the engineers is selected to make rounds in the engine room during the night. This sys- tem allows concentration of the workforce during longer runs and is quite efficient. It isn't, however, very suitable for Great Lakes trading.

In the early 1950s, a marine engineer's union, known as the Brotherhood of Marine Engineers, introduced a set of wellness programs into their contracts with shipping companies. These programs were unheard of in an industry where the company had always wielded the power, even though seaman's unions had been active since the 1800s. These plans included a pension fund, paid health care, and family leave.

A very strong owners' association blocked the introduction of these plans for many years on the Great Lakes, but as the unions gained momentum on both coasts, they eventually made their appearance in Great Lakes contracts. With the family leave program, centuries of history of mariners being forced to choose between a job or a life ashore came to an end. By the late 1980s, the family leave program allowed for thirty days paid leave after sixty days aboard the vessel for Great Lakes contracts. For deep sea contracts, sailors got sixty days leave for 120 days onboard.

While the 60/30 plan is still the most common on the Lakes, some contracts allow for "day-for-day" paid time off the vessel. Others provide three-quarters for one program. The Lakes contracts I sailed were the 60/30 type, and deep-sea the 120/60 type. However, in 1991, during the first Gulf War, deep-sea mariners were in short supply, and a relief was nearly impossible to find.

Generally, I didn't mind the time aboard ship, all before cell phones and email. I would get a routine established: stand my watch, take care of laundry and such, read and study for my next exam. I was quite happy. It takes a particular personality to adapt to the isolation, and truthfully the 4-8 watch was the best in my mind because nobody was around to bother you while you were on watch, at least most of the time.

Samuel Johnson is quoted as saying: "No man will be a sailor who has contrivance enough to get himself into a jail; for being in a ship is being in a jail, with the chance of being drowned … A man in a jail has more room, better food, and commonly better company." However, I would disagree. I have never been to jail, so I may be mistaken. Sailors tend to use that quote to describe their life.

In June of 1987, I was hired by Skaarup Lakes Shipping, the operating company for the Huron cement boats, as they transitioned to Inland Lakes Management control. The pay scale wasn't what I hoped for, but shipping was slow at that time, and I was happy to be working. Even so, these cement boat jobs were nice! The crews had been together for years, and most lived in Alpena, Michigan. They were like family—and a lot of them were related in one way or another. The plants were well maintained with very few problems. The quarters were good, and the galley crews did an outstanding job.

We had dining rooms for officers and crew where the officers were required to have a clean, collared shirt on to sit at the table. The menu would be posted, and a mess steward or porter would take your order and bring your food to the dining room. During heavy weather, the tablecloth would be dampened to keep your china plate from sliding around, and the tables had a trim piece that could be raised as well. The ships carried a Steward, who was the head of the galley department, a second cook, who was a baker. We always had fresh bread, cookies, biscuits, cakes, and pies. There were porters and a night cook who would do prep work and make the night lunch for the evening and early morning watches. With the longer unloading times, good ports, easy-to-run machinery, and great people, it was enjoyable work.

JOB DESCRIPTIONS

Job descriptions on the Great Lakes and deep-sea ships have changed over the past fifty years, with ship automation and the switch to diesel power for many ships. However, because the ships on the Great Lakes can last seventy-five years (and in a few cases over a hundred years), the boiler-related jobs have continued on the Great Lakes much longer than on those newer, diesel-powered, deep-sea ships. Many steam boiler ships are still operating on the Great Lakes.

TYPICAL JOBS

Here is a list of the typical jobs on a steam-powered, Great Lakes ore carrier. These may also apply to the car ferries, other than where noted:

> **Navigation crew (aka forward end)**—The navigation crew consists of the captain, first mate, second mate, third mate, three wheelsmen, bos'n—though not on every ship—three deck watchmen, sometimes a deck maintenance man—all considered Able-Bodied Seamen—and two or three deckhands. All but the deckhands are required to have Coast Guard certificates.

> **Engine room crew (aka after end)**—The engine room crew is made up of the chief engineer, first engineer, second engineer, third engineer, three oilers, three firemen, three coal passers, and one wiper. On the car ferries, they also have a watertender, working in the engine room but watching boiler operation.

> The firemen, coal passers, and watertender are only needed on ships with steam propulsion. Some diesel-powered ships may have three oilers.

> **Galley crew**—The galley crew includes the steward, first cook, and two porters. Some of the newer ships have only a chief cook and second cook.

The self-unloading ships also carry one conveyor man and one gateman considered part of the engineering crew, although some companies have the gateman in the deck crew. They are only needed during unloading, but they also maintain the conveyor system each day when the ship is in transit.

SHIP DESIGN

The cargo ships themselves are very different in the Great Lakes. Ships evolved over the last 150 years from short, rigid ships to sleek ships with sharp, pointed bows, and then to the boxy, blunt-nosed ships of today. The old ships lasted a long time, a few as long as a hundred years. Many were retired because their propulsion systems wore out, and it was not economically feasible to repower them. The new ships are more efficient and carry up to ten times the cargo as the old ones, but they don't have the same style. Self-unloading ships were introduced very early on the Great Lakes, and today most ships have been converted to self-unloaders. Money and profit win over aesthetics every time.

Two big structural differences I'd say in the old designs were the cargo holds and the deck naming system. The main deck on the pre-1970 ore carrier was *not* the top weather deck as seen from the outside. Technically, the top deck on those older Great Lakes freighters was the spar deck. If you look up the definition of spar deck, it is "an upper deck of light construction, above the main deck" per the *Design & Construction of Steel Vessels*.

That definition seems implausible unless you go inside the cargo hold of the ship. The pre-1940 vessel had a ledge along the sides of the cargo holds, where one could access the ballast tanks of the ship. That ledge was the main deck and it provided both strength and watertight compartmentation to the ship. Although the deck plate, or deck stringer, outside the cargo hatches was heavy, the deck between and around the cargo hatches was much lighter. Thus, the top deck was a spar deck.

1940- to 1970-built vessels enclosed the area around that ledge on each side. This created a weathertight and dust-free tunnel, extending from the forward deckhouse, back to the engineering spaces. This made it easier for the deck crew to access the galley. The ledge on the main deck of those older ships was dirty, unlighted, and dangerous to walk, unless for maintenance. It was covered by cargo dust and walking there was a chore. But the 1940s version was clean, well lit, and well protected from the bad weather.

The ship structure changed dramatically in the 1970s. Most ships began to place the pilothouse aft and the entire crew was berthed in the single after deckhouse. The spar deck also became a thing of the past on these new ships. The ballast tanks extend to the top deck, making that top deck the main deck.

The origin of the "forward end" and "aft end" designation for crew members comes from that old design, with two deckhouses. You can see where this forward-ender and aft-ender terminology came from by looking at the old Lake freighters with a forward deckhouse where the pilothouse and crew's quarters were located for the navigation officers and deck crew. The aft end of the vessel had a deckhouse over the engine room, with quarters for the engineering officers and engine room crew.

The engineers also benefited from the galley crew and dining rooms being located aft, probably due to the reduced motion aft. Increased comfort during meals and fewer broken dishes during storms probably contributed to that design decision. This was different on deep-sea cargo ships, which typically had one deckhouse in those days, near the center of the ship, for both the navigation and engineering crew. Modern deep-sea vessels have the deckhouse aft.

The design of Great Lakes ships has changed over the years. Because some of the ships were thought to be structurally insufficient during the late 1800s to early 1900s, the whaleback freighter design was developed. The idea was to allow the waves to wash over the deck, reducing the shock load on the hull sides. The whalebacks were small and carried much less cargo, so they were not used very long. Some whalebacks were built as barges with no propulsion machinery. Others became barges when their machinery failed or became obsolete.

There were two different designs of whalebacks. One design was called the "pig boat," due to the flat-nosed bow. It also had a very small, rounded pilothouse. You'll see in the photo titled "Whaleback at the Soo Locks" in the back of the chapter is leaving the old Poe Lock at the Soo before that lock was enlarged in the mid-1960s.

The next photo shows a whaleback which had a more conventional bow and pilothouse. But it still had the whaleback hull. That picture is a vessel departing Duluth, Minnesota. The postcard was mailed and postmarked in Duluth in June 1919.

If you look at the pictures in Chapter 11 will see a picture of the *Christopher Columbus*, which was a whaleback converted to a passenger excursion vessel. It brought passengers to the World's Columbian Exposition in Chicago in 1893. It also had a pig-nose design.

THE JOB CAN BE DANGEROUS

My father once told me about an accident that occurred during the winter lay-up, where a ship's engineer had been under a boiler, performing maintenance. Something happened that allowed steam to fill the bilges beneath the boiler. The engineer died.

Work on ships was always dangerous, and in addition to accidental deaths, there were many deaths caused by cancers and lung problems, traceable to the work done on these ships. After my father died in 1978, just seven years after he retired, I received a call from the University of Minnesota, which was doing a study on industrial deaths. They asked if I could answer a few questions about my father's industrial death. I told them my father had died of natural causes—congestive heart failure—but agreed to answer their questions.

The questions went something like this: Did your father work around coal dust? What about silica (sand) dust? Oils containing PCBs? Smoke or oil fumes? Asbestos? And the clincher was carbon tetrachloride. Hell, my father washed his greasy hands in carbon tet, and so did I back in the 1960s!

So, then the interviewer asked, "Do you still think your father died of totally natural causes?"

I remember my father coming home the year the *Daniel J. Morrell* sank. He had been very upset because his ship was also on Lake Huron during that storm. His captain had been more conservative and had sought shelter. My father had been with many captains who would not seek shelter or even slow down in a storm, but he said he was "lucky with this year's captain." My mother tried to use this to persuade my dad to find a shore job, but within a few weeks, he was anxiously waiting for the phone call, telling him when and where to report to his next ship.

TROUBLE AT A LOADING PORT

Captain Aaron Menough is a Great Lakes pilot and Aaron has written some interesting stories about his career on Great Lakes freighters. Many of his stories are long and interesting, but they are too long for this book. Therefore, Aaron graciously gave me the right to pick and choose and edit his stories as necessary.

His first story describes the start of his interest in becoming a merchant mariner. It also touches on his doubts about that decision, after he was knocked unconscious during an accident while working on deck.

Like many high school graduates, Aaron was not ready for college—I was one of those, too—so he left Toledo, Ohio, and joined the Navy. He served on the U.S.S. *Kitty Hawk* aircraft carrier. He was chosen for an interview in the ship's newspaper, and amongst other answers that got him in trouble he mentioned his favorite city was Traverse City, Michigan, where his family had spent summer vacations. He had always enjoyed the city.

When he returned from the Navy, he showed that ship's newspaper article to his dad and they decided to go back to Traverse City for a visit. His father pulled into the parking lot of a college—probably trying to aim Aaron toward a good career—and Aaron picked up some brochures. He was surprised to see the college had a maritime academy, but he still was not thinking about college.

After returning home, working a construction job in the cold of winter, Aaron looked for those brochures he had gathered. He filled out an application for the Great Lakes Maritime Academy. He was accepted and became a third mate on a Great Lakes freighter.

Aaron's story not only provides insight into the tough work at some docks but describes an accident that rendered him unconscious:

As a child, growing up in Toledo, Ohio, I never would've pictured myself going to work on a Great Lakes freighter. I was twenty miles from the lake; my dad frequently took me to Marblehead to watch the ships load, just like all the other kids. But to step foot on a real working freighter was a rare opportunity. Then to watch them leave the dock and shrink off into the distance, that was mystical.

But here I am today, lying on my back. That's how I landed. It's six thirty in the morning—still dark out. It's quiet. I can taste a grand mixture of blood, salt, and limestone. I'm fairly sure my front teeth are missing or turned around. I think I've just been hit by a car. Something about a Great Lakes freighter I start to remember; I feel the hatch clamp dig into my leg. I try to stand up but I'm under the unloading boom. It's only five feet high. I'm six foot four.

The next thing I know, it's 7:30 a.m., and I'm in the galley.

"How did I get here?" I ask Irene, our cook.

"You don't remember?" she asks.

"I went to turn on a winch, ran back across the other side, stooped down to get under the unloading boom, and now I'm in the galley," I say.

It turns out my teeth aren't missing after all, just chipped off. "You're gonna have to go to the hospital honey," Irene says. She was trying to play nurse for me.

I can't believe this is happening.

We had just finished loading ten thousand tons of salt at the Morton Salt dock in Fairport, Ohio. This place is incredibly challenging. There is no dock face to tie along, so we have to send the deckhands out in a little twelve-foot aluminum boat, dragging nylon lines behind them for about 150 feet through poison ivy, snakes, jagged rocks, and rusted rebar. Once ashore, two guys have to drag a one-inch steel cable across the water. It always seems to happen at 2:00 a.m., in pitch black, and the boat is always drifting away in the wind, making the cable pull even harder. If you're lucky, the nylon lines won't break halfway across the water. Even when you do get done tying up to the Morton dock, the loading rig is so rickety and old, you're lucky just to get the salt near the right hatch. A guy comes out of what looks like a treehouse from the 1950s and swivels an aluminum spout over us. Then you spend the next fourteen hours with road salt blowing in your face and dowsing all the equipment.

I was working on deck that night, and I tucked, turned, and ducked around my opponents. In this case, it was the steel unloading boom. I had to start the winch motor, which is on the starboard side of the ship because there are no controls on the port side where we were mooring. All I had to do was sprint over from the port side of the ship and run the controls. That is the last thing I remember.

Flip to the end of the chapter to see the boom that Aaron tried to get under.

And check out the control area on the opposite side of the ship, where Aaron was headed.

Had I not mentioned Traverse City in that Navy newspaper questionnaire, my dad never would've read it, we never would've gone up to Traverse City, and I never would've grabbed those brochures. I never would've completed the Academy or received my license, and eventually, and most importantly, I might not have run full speed into that unloading boom, on a ship that was built in 1929.

An that's how I got here.

SOME HISTORY

During World War II, the deep-sea merchant vessels tended to have a Coast Guard or sometimes a Navy complement of men aboard, manning guns on deck. Because the Great Lakes were not in danger of enemy fire from aircraft or U-boats, the war department decided to designate the officers onboard the Great Lakes cargo vessels as Reserve Coast Guard officers, all second lieutenants (aka lieutenant JGs). As soon as the war ended, their commission also ended. None of these sailors received any compensation, other than a uniform allowance, and they received no veterans' benefits.

The officers only wore these uniforms when they went ashore. During working hours, they wore their normal, civilian-type work clothing.

Flip to the end of the chapter to see my mother and father. He is wearing the Coast Guard uniform during shore leave. The couple was on their honeymoon in 1943.

Flip to the end of the chapter to see the discharge book. All sailors carried a discharge book, showing their sign-on and sign-off dates from each ship, signed by each captain on those ships. This one belonged to Matt Ojala.

1. U.S. Gypsum, typical Great Lakes self-unloader.

2. Whaleback at the Soo Locks.

3. Whaleback down bound in Duluth.

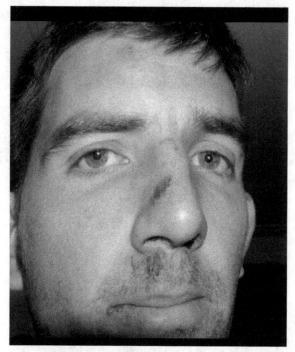

4. Captain Aaron's mashed nose from accident.

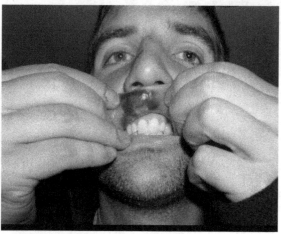

5. Captain Aaron's battered lip.

6. Unloading boom which caused Aaron's damage.

7. One of very few women deckhands on freighters.

8. Matt Ojala and other officers in Coast Guard uniform.

41

9. Matt Ojala, author's father, in uniform during WWII.

10. Matt Ojala's Discharge Book, 1937–1970.

CHAPTER 3

_____

Great Lakes Maintenance

Another difference between deep-sea and Great Lakes ships is that on Great Lakes ships, crews do much of the maintenance on machinery, deck equipment, and minor repairs other than hull welding. Although somewhat of a generalization, deep-sea ships tend to have shipyards or other shore-based maintenance crews do such work, except for some of the smaller, coastal shipping companies.

Partly because of the winter lay-up status of many Great Lakes ships, the crew performs their major repairs, usually during the winter. Many of the crew also want the extra income from this work. This not only increased their pay, but it also extended their time away from home.

The following example, including the three photographs, happened on the car ferry the *Badger*. The low-pressure (LP) piston on one of the main propulsion steam engines needed to be overhauled and the crew did all the work themselves. Steam engine pistons are not small, as seen in the first photo. It required a lot of rigging to get the piston out of the engine and then out of the ship.

Flip to the end of the chapter, which shows several of the crew, including Mike Braybrook and Chief Chuck Cart, inside the steam engine crankcase during the removal of that piston, as shown on the one of the other photos.

One of the other photos shows the LP piston, looking up from inside the crankcase.·

THE WORKERS

Although it is getting harder to find young men and women who will stick with these jobs, those who do eventually become dedicated, work hard, and complain little—except to their families.

Some of the jobs aboard ship are dirty. The boiler room is a hot place to work and still keep a smile on your face. Some of the photos at the end of the chapter show some of the engine crew at work on a coal-fired, steam car ferry. We show one of the men twice. Once with a clean T-shirt at the start of his shift and once at the end of his shift.·'''

Jim Fay, a Great Lakes shipping historian, contributed a photo taken in the 1930's, showing a similar scene of a fireman stoking a boiler. At least on the coal-fired steamships, not much has changed.

THE OLD AND THE NEW

One of the major differences in the engine rooms, besides the changes from steam to diesel propulsion systems, is the modern control rooms in the engine room. See the photos at the end of the chapter, showing the watch engineer standing next to the engines, with the controls. The engine order telegraph was also located there. One of those photos, shows my father, Matt Ojala, standing watch in the engine room.

However, even the steamships improved the working comfort for the watch engineers. They did so by placing the engine controls in an air-conditioned control room as shown in one of the photos.

There is a picture showing a wheelsman on the carferry *Badger*. The wheelsman's sole job while on watch is to steer the vessel (whether in open water or in port and during docking). They learn to anticipate the captain's or the mate's wishes, but they respond to the orders given to them. Responding quickly is important. The job may get boring on long runs, but they need to stay focused.

I personally acted as a wheelsman on only one occasion, while serving in the Coast Guard. The experience was necessary as part of a rate qualification. After one four-hour watch, I was happy it was not part of my normal duties. I had been tense the whole time!

THE ACCIDENTAL WHEELSMAN: A MIKE BRAYBROOK STORY

The following story was given to me by Mike Braybrook, and it looks like his experience was similar:

Back in the late 1970s, I had a relief oiler job on the car ferry City of Milwaukee *for several weeks. I got off the 8:00 p.m.–12:00 a.m. watch, and I came up out of the engine room. I went to the flicker to clean up and then went up to the galley for lunch. I even still recall what I had: the cook was serving his signature BLTs, which were among the best I've ever had.*

It was an unusually warm day for early spring, so I thought I would take a walk up the deck and stop by the wheelhouse for a visit. We were due at the Muskegon break wall in about half an hour. Coming into the wheelhouse, I found Bud at the wheel, and the mate was in the front window enjoying the breeze.

After a bit of small talk, Bud smiled and said, "Hey, I could use a break. Wanna take the wheel for a bit?"

I said, "Sure, why not?"

I had some clue about how to wheel, because I had some experience wheeling on my Navy tanker, on the "trick" wheel located down in the steering gear room. Bud walked over by the open front window where the mate was standing and started shooting the bull. I enjoyed steering, as it was a calm day, and only needed one or two degrees of rudder to keep her on course.

When we were about fifteen minutes from the break wall, the captain came up to the wheelhouse to take her into the harbor. He smiled and said, "I see we have a new wheelsman," as he went over to talk to the mate.

As we got closer to the wall, I expected Bud to come back and take over any minute. But he seemed content to hang out by the front windows with the captain and mate. I was getting a bit nervous, as we were almost to the break walls, when the captain nonchalantly said, "Put her right down the middle." All I could say was, "Down the middle, aye, Cap."

So, while the three of them continued with their small talk, I tried to keep her down the middle. We passed through the outer harbor and approached the channel, where I thought for sure the wheelsman would reclaim his wheel. But no, he stayed where he was, engrossed in conversation.

When passing through a restricted waterway, like a channel, the rudder doesn't respond the same as in open water, unbeknownst to me at the time. As we traveled through, the boat slowly started to go a bit sideways. I gave the wheel another turn thinking that would bring her back straight, but she continued to slip sideways. Now I'm getting nervous, as she wasn't answering up like she should!

Finally, Bud turned around and said, "Well, I guess we don't want to run her into the wall." He laughed as he came and took over the wheel, much to my relief. When he did, he spun it and she slowly but surely came back straight.

"You need to put twice as much wheel on when moving through a tight waterway like the channel," he then told me.

Now you tell me, I thought.

All the while, the Captain was as calm as could be.

This may be a good time to define the word *flicker*, which Mike used in the above story. Apparently, there are two definitions.

The first one, which I had always heard, is as follows:

On Great Lakes car ferries, the engine crew's berthing area was aft of the engine room, beneath the car deck. The car deck had the railroad track mounted on deck, where the train cars were loaded. The vibration from the railcars on that deck caused the lights in this berthing area to flicker, which gave it that name.

Although Mike had also heard my definition, he also heard a second definition, which also makes sense:

> The early electric dynamos were running at forty cycles so that the cycles were visible in the lighting. There were no portholes down in the flicker, so all they had was artificial light, unlike the forward staterooms. So, the flicker name could have come from those earlier ferries, built around the turn of the century, with those forty-cycle electric lights.

LAKE ORE BOATS - DECK DEPARTMENT

We have not described the ore carriers' forward-enders jobs in good detail so far in this book. Just like engineers, jobs have evolved over the years. Some of the job changes came from changes in the ship designs, like the switch from boilers to diesel machinery. Other changes were to save money on crew salary costs. Manpower was cheap in the early days, so having different crewmen for each task was not a problem. However, because of the competition from tugs pushing barges, many as large as ore carriers, the shipping companies had to cut costs to stay competitive.

Captain Ed Wiltse offers a great description of the various deck department rates with some job definitions. He also addresses changes in the crew, which has evolved over the years:

> *Ordinary seaman (OS) deckhand is the entry rate. After 360 days of sea time and the successful completion of the Coast Guard's Able-Bodied Seaman (AB) exam, an OS becomes an AB and can fill any AB position in the crew. Some ABs prefer to steer, and usually work into AB watchstander jobs, which was previously called the wheelsman. Other guys prefer to*

stay out on deck, and those usually promote to AB bos'n or AB maintenance jobs.

Deck watches were gone before I started sailing in 1985. The guys said they had the easiest job on the ship. All the deck watch needed to do was make coffee and call the watch.

AB watchmen were still around for a while. Underway, they would work with the deckhands, rinsing down, or on some painting projects. At night, they would do sanitary duties inside the accommodations, hallways, stairwells, and so forth. They would relieve the wheelsmen for coffee breaks and wake the watch. The watchmen went away in the early 1990s.

After the AB watchmen position went away, there was usually only one AB on watch to wheel, stand lookout, do sanitary, or whatever was needed. They cover any other duties needed during the watch, by paying overtime to the off-duty ABs.

The AB wheelsmen are now called AB watchstanders, and are only stationed in the pilothouse during those times sailing in restricted waters (rivers, harbors and narrow channels), during maneuvering, or any other occasion as deemed necessary. Otherwise, they are usually working down on deck.

As for the AB bos'n, most ships do still carry a bos'n. They are more or less the foreman of the deck gang. However, not many of the old-time bos'ns still exist today. One of the best was my friend who sailed for the Great Lakes fleet out of Rogers City and spent the last number of years as the bos'n on the John G. Munson. He is probably the last, and best, example of the real old-school bos'ns, who you likely remember. He was a huge man, but a gentle giant. However, when he was on the job, he was quite the imposing figure for the deckhands. He always led by example. See the photo of the crew pulling tarps, at the end if this chapter.

That picture shows deckhands pulling tarps off the old-style, telescoping hatch covers. Those hatch covers had to be tarped—covered by heavy tarpaulin—many times with two layers, particularly when carrying grain cargoes. During the fall, winter, and spring months, the hatches were covered for safety. Those hatches were not watertight, just weathertight.

Another photo is from the 1937 collection, provided by Jim Fay. It shows the deck crew working on the telescoping hatch clamps. There is also a photo from Mike Braybrook, showing the deck crew working on opening the telescoping hatch.

The deckhands still remove the hatch clamps to be ready for loading or unloading cargo, then they replace the clamps and/or tarps when leaving port. But today's job is easier, because the one-piece hatch covers are watertight—not needing tarps—and they are removed by a rolling deck crane that is specifically designed to lift and move the hatch covers in one piece. However, many of the deck crew jobs have been eliminated or combined to reduce the size of the crew.

DECKHANDS

The engine room jobs can be hot and dirty, but what about the deckhands? They are up in the clean air and get to watch the scenery along the Lakes, and even ogle the girls on the yachts going by.

It sounds like they have it made, but then you haven't heard the rest of the story! The deckhands are awakened before they reach each dock, and then landed on bos'n chairs to handle lines on the dock. It is just a wood plank connected to a rope. These photos shown in the back of the chapter are relatively recent. The use of the bos'n chair is not a thing of the past.

When transiting the locks at the Soo, or the St. Lawrence Seaway, the deckhands also have to be on deck, and on the lock wall, handling lines.

Of course, this is not only done in great, sunny weather, with a light breeze caressing their face. The crews work in all weather, rain, snow, ice, and dangerous conditions. The good captains don't allow the deck crew to be on deck when the waves could wash them overboard, but there were instances of that happening, back in the old days.

The deck crew, sometimes run by a bos'n, also does all of the deck cleaning, painting, and minor maintenance. Cargo spilled during loading and unloading has to be shoveled or washed away. The vessel also has to be painted, inside and out, so the deck crew is quite busy.

It was and is a tough job! Yet many of those guys kept sailing!

COAL RUN IN LAKE ERIE – AN ED WILTSE STORY

This next story is from Captain Ed Wiltse about his contract on a Great Lakes ore boat, on the coal run from Toledo to nearby Monroe, Michigan. Ed graduated from GLMA, but he was not able to get an officer's job straight out of school, so he worked with the deck crew for one summer:

> *After I graduated from GLMA in '87, there were no jobs, so I shipped out as a deckhand for a few months on the S.S. Armco for Columbia Transportation.*
>
> *I remember we were on the coal shuttle from Toledo to Monroe, in the heat of August that summer. It was a very hot summer that year, especially down on Lake Erie. I can remember the heat caused a steamy haze on the lake, so the shoreline or the other ships appeared distorted. The other memorable part of this story was that because the Armco was a 1950s vintage steamer, the forward end was not air-conditioned.*
>
> *Ships that did the coal shuttle on western Lake Erie had an exemption to leave their hatches off, and they would pile the coal over the top of the coamings, and out onto the deck between the hatches. The coal was everywhere, and of course, it was the deckhand's job to shovel the coal back into the hatches while the ship was unloading.*
>
> *Shoveling coal all day in the summer sun down on western Lake Erie was hot, grueling work, even though I was only in my early twenties back then. The coal dust would stick to you while you sweat. It got into your nose; you could feel the grit between your teeth; it got in your ears. It was everywhere.*

And the spiders loved coal. They came aboard with the cargo—hundreds of them! Big honkin' spiders, hanging everywhere ... under every overhang, under every deck light, in the windlass room. Just everywhere.

So, after shoveling coal all day, we were so filthy, so disgusting, we would take a wash-down hose, and hose each other off on top of a hatch cover, rather than go inside the accommodations and track grimy coal dirt inside. Each guy would strip down to his shorts and would get a bar of soap to lather up for the hose down.

Later, when it was time to sleep, the inside of the ship would stay hot. It felt like the inside of an oven. Sometimes you couldn't open your porthole. If the ship was loading, the coal dust in the air came through the portholes. Even if the ship was underway and you could open your porthole, the humid Lake Erie air wasn't much of a relief.

The most effective way to cool down so you could sleep was to take a cool shower and, while still wet, lie down on your bunk on top of the sheets. You then laid a wet towel on your chest. With a fan blowing on you, the wet towel acting as a heat exchanger would keep you cool—at least for a while. You would be wet when you lay down to sleep and, when you woke up, you were usually wet with sweat, lying on wet sheets. You never dried out. It was a constant cycle of sweat to wet, to sweat again.

It was tough to work on those Lake Erie coal runs, particularly on those old ships. But they were memorable times. I wonder how young people today would deal with hardship like that. Would they do it without question like we did? I don't know.

There is a photo at the end of this chapter, showing a crewman washing down the spar deck after the cargo was loaded. The excess cargo spilled on deck is dangerous. So, this wash down is done after each loading and unloading operation. In winter, those hoses are used with hot water to remove ice on the deck. It is one of those hoses that deckhands used to clean themselves after a tough day shoveling coal in Captain Wiltse's story.

Also notice that those are the one-piece hatch covers in that photo, which replaced the old telescoping covers. However, the hatch clamps still have to be removed before and after loading, and also before and after unloading.

LAKE ORE BOATS - ENGINEERS

One of the more interesting engineers we met while working on this book is Katrina (Kat) Walheim. She doesn't quite fit the picture most might imagine of a "grease monkey" aboard a Lakes freighter.

Katrina Walheim is an engineering graduate of the Great Lakes Maritime Academy, and she has been sailing as an engineer since 2012. She is now a first engineer and has enough time to sit for her chief engineer's license. She wants to get more experience before making that next move. The following comments are from Kat:

> I went to GLMA. When I was starting in my class, there were seven female cadets. I started on the deck side of things and ended up switching to the engineering side during my second semester at the Academy. I feel like everyone sees the glamour on the deck side of the industry, but I found the engineering side much more interesting. When I switched to the engineering side, I had no prior mechanical experience whatsoever, so to think of that, and where I am now, it's kind of funny. Surprisingly, none of my family had anything to do with the maritime industry. I ended up in the academy on a whim because I had no idea what I wanted to major in at college. I met some of the maritime guys at the community college in Traverse City who suggested I try sailing. My dad called me crazy at first for wanting to sail, but now he and my mom are super supportive and brag about me all the time.

My first cadet ship was the American Mariner, *and I stood watch with Sue [Lieblein] and Lori [Reinhart]. Lori ended up boarding the vessel about a month or so into my cadet sea project. So, I guess I got kind of lucky, in the fact that there were other females on my first shipping experience. Despite that, I hated my first cadet sea project and was thinking about quitting the Academy. I stuck with it, though, and it wasn't until my second sea project with Great Lakes Fleet (GLF), on the* Cason J. Callaway, *that I enjoyed myself. At some companies, the crews seemed to be a little more "licensed versus unlicensed," and you could see the divide because the crew's and the officer's galleys were separate. At GLF, the crew seemed to be one big family. I guess I'm generalizing from my own experience, but when I go to ships from other companies, it still seems to be like that. I guess that's probably a big reason why I remained sailing for GLF instead.*

As far as advancement goes, I have never had problems in that area. I think I got into the industry at a good time. A lot of people were retiring, so I moved up fast. I sailed out of the union hall with AMO, for about two years before I was offered the permanent third engineer job on the Philip R. Clarke *in 2014. I've been there ever since. I got the second assistant's job a year or so after, and then when I got my first assistant engineer's license, I got the permanent first assistant job right away. I have enough time to send in for my chief's license, but I'm kind of dragging my feet on it because I feel like I need a little more experience before I get thrown into that position. Right now, the industry is hurting for the higher licenses, and if I got my chief's license, I would be relief chief as soon as it was in my hands.*

As far as my reasons go for being attracted to sailing, I'd be lying if I didn't say the paycheck was a factor. I also like how each day is different out here, especially for engineers. There is always something to work on, and I learn something new every day. The job is very gratifying for me. The scenery is also nice and being able to get off the ship in the different ports breaks up the monotony as well. That is one of the reasons why I like being on the smaller ships versus the big ones. We go to a lot more ports, and we are usually in port every few days.

I think the vessel's crew plays a huge part in why sailors decide to stay on certain vessels as well. Personally, I get along well with both the deck and the engine crew on my boat. At first, I think they were kind of leery of me. Once they found out I could swear and joke around with the rest of them, I was golden. Being on the same boat all the time also helps because the crew is used to me. If another female comes aboard, they usually are a little bit more reserved at first, until they get to know her.

Getting respect has not been a problem. I don't think it's any different from other jobs. As long as people see that you can do your job, and do it well, then you will eventually gain respect. In being a first assistant, my chief expects me to assign jobs to all the other engineers, and unlicensed crew. So not only does my crew see me doing my job, but I'm involved in most of what they do as well. Especially in the engine room, we must operate as a team, and everyone has their strengths and weaknesses to offer to that team. So if everyone is working together, we all respect each other more.

I've sailed with other women on various ships. In fact, I've had two separate female captains. My first job as a third engineer was on an ocean vessel, and the captain on that ship was a female in her thirties. I've sailed with Lori as my captain a great number of times because we are both permanent crew on the same vessel. There have also been a few female relief mates who have been on the ships I've sailed on, and lots of cooks and second cooks are female.

You don't seem to see as many unlicensed females on the deck or engine side, though. I think in the eight years I've been *sailing, I've only run into two or three unlicensed deck females, and maybe one or two unlicensed engine room ladies. For some reason, I think they may be more prevalent in the oceans. The guys always joke there shouldn't be more than one female per department, because it would cause catfights. But I do wish I had more opportunities to sail with other females. It would be nice to have girl talk occasionally.*

As far as relationships go, I have not been married yet, but I've had a few boyfriends while sailing. Relationships out here can be tough because you don't get to see each other every day.

Family and friends are always super supportive. I have lost touch with a few friends, but most of my friends understand what I do and are just happy to hang out with me when I'm home. The first few years of sailing were kind of lonely, but I think the longer you sail, the more you get into the routine of it, and it gets better. Wi-Fi and FaceTime help us to keep in touch with friends and family at home, so that's nice too.

On my vessel and within our fleet, I feel as though our camaraderie is high. If two of our boats are in the same port, it's nice to go "up the street" and see coworkers you may not have seen in a while. Even if we can't make it uptown, sometimes we can just hop on the other boat and visit the guys down in the engine room or on deck while they're on watch. I try to get off the boat as much as possible, and usually I'm not by myself. At lay-up or fit-out time, most of the engine room crew goes uptown together, either to eat or to go to the bar, or even bowling. During the sailing season, it's more limited, but we still try to go uptown together once in a while, depending on the watch schedules. Going up with the guys from the engine room is usually funny because it will normally be me and like five or six older guys, who act more like crazy uncles than coworkers.

Again, the stories received from the female engineers in these Great Lakes ore carriers are very interesting. The following comes from Joyce Estelle. Joyce is an engineering graduate of GLMA, and she has her chief engineer's license. She sails on one of the fleets of ore carriers, serving the steel mills. Sailing as an engineer is a second career for Joyce, as you will see in her story. See some of the photos of Joyce at work, at the end of this chapter.

My sailing career started on the Trump Casino *in Gary, Indiana. I took the job only after not getting called from the union hiring hall after several months, and I needed to start making money. It was like a glorified janitorial job, but it paid great! I stayed for six years. But when that dried up, I came to the Lakes for a couple of thirty-day relief jobs before the end of the season. I then took a job on a paddle wheeler on the Mississippi River and worked with a mean, condescending chief engineer who treated me terribly. Three of the four engineers were female.*

On one occasion, the chief got in my face and told me to "shut the @#&! up and keep quiet" unless I was spoken to. The chief was the type that could have made my life miserable. As I was job searching, Hurricane Katrina smashed into New Orleans, which bankrupted the company. We were all let go. That's when I came back to the Lakes and sailed as a relief engineer for a year or so on a variety of boats. I was hired by my current company in the spring of 2007, where I've been ever since.

Sailing is a tough industry. It's like living inside a commercial factory with motors and engines and ventilation noises constantly in your ear. The boats are never still, even while tied up in port. There's always some sort of vibration or noise. In fact, when I go home, it takes a couple of days to get used to a dead quiet, motionless environment. And as an engineer, we are constantly feeling the movement of the ship and listening for changes in how things sound, which tell us when something is wrong, even from our staterooms. So we never get away from our job.

The hardest thing I find about sailing is that we don't ever get a day off. Officers typically work sixty or ninety days in a row without a day off. Then we get a month off, which is wonderful. But during those days at work, we don't ever get a break. I would love to have a couple of days a month to just unwind and not think.

The captains and chief engineers are on call 24/7, but they can adjust their day to allow for a solid night of sleep. If you are standing a watch, you work the weird—and very tiring—four hours on, then eight hours off. Then repeat. So, we go to work twice a day, for four hours. Add in the time it takes to eat, take a shower, and unwind a bit, and you're hard-pressed to put together more than four or six hours of sleep. That's the other thing that I find hard.

Another thing about shipboard life: we are a floating city, with our own fire department, water department, electric department, hospital—loosely defined—restaurant, fitness center, library, and movie theater (with HBO, Cinemax, and every other channel you can imagine with satellite TV). We run twenty-four hours a day, we don't stop for weekends, and we don't stop at 5:00 p.m.[26, 27, 28]

As a woman, you get tested. I've never been challenged to the point of harassment, but guys—especially the older ones who were raised with the "women stay at home" mentality— will hold you to a higher standard. And the first piece of advice I was given, while I was still at the Academy in Traverse City, was one I've carried with me my entire career: If you can do the job on your own two feet without the help of someone, you'll be fine, and you'll be accepted as one of the crew. If you're afraid to try things, if you're afraid to break a nail, or if you're constantly asking for help, you turn into a hindrance for the other crew members, who have their own jobs to do. You don't need to be Xena, warrior princess, but you also can't be a delicate little flower.

My first job on my license, I was terrified! I was an engineer, yes, but I didn't have the experience under my belt to have a grasp on everything. A chief engineer told me once that I didn't have to know it all right away. If I observed, asked good questions, and had a desire to succeed, everything would fall into place.

He also said, "Don't worry about knowing exactly what to do when the shit hits the fan. When something big goes wrong, you won't be alone for long." He was right. It was a comforting feeling to know that people smarter than me were coming down from their rooms to help out.

I nearly quit the company I currently work for during my first year, thirteen years ago. There were a couple of people in the engine department that blamed me for everything that went wrong, and some of it was nitpicky stuff, like putting a tool away in the wrong place. But one of the engineers pulled me aside one day and said I was doing a great job, and not to let those jerks push me around. He liked my work ethic and said I was just a threat to those other guys. I don't know if that's true or not, but I appreciated his belief in me, and to this day, he's one of my best friends, even though he's no longer sailing.

But now I'm the permanent first engineer and relief chief engineer. I'm nearly at the top of the ladder but I'm still learning. And I'm not in competition with anyone except myself.

I also want to add that this industry is not for anyone with thin skin, men or women. Some sailors are rough around the edges and can spew cuss words and vulgarities almost as a normal part of their conversation. And dirty jokes still exist, even in today's world of political correctness. More than a handful of times, I've heard guys out here say that sailors are just weird enough that they don't do well in normal society. I have known a couple of people who have fit that description, but most are just everyday guys, doing a job that requires us to be away from our loved ones to make a good living.

Until a person comes out here and tries this job, they will never understand just how difficult it can be, working every single day we're here, being away from our families, and being out of communication much of the time. We can't socialize with friends. Sometimes we don't get off the ship to go uptown for a haircut, supplies, or other reasons, since we are often only in port for six to eight hours. If it's during our working hours, we have to be on the ship. If we're in port during our off-hours, we may not have time to go "up the street," and if we do, we best not miss the boat!

1. Carferry Badger crew after removing piston

2. Carferry Badger crew working inside the steam engine

3. The piston, as seen from below, inside the crankcase

4. Coal-fired Carferry firemen; a very dirty job

5. A happy coalpasser in the boiler room

6. Fireman with great tattoos

7. Great smiles, at the start of their shift.

8. They look a little dirtier at the end of the shift.

9. Fireman on duty, back in the old days.

10. Old style control station.

11. Matt Ojala, author's father, on watch in the engine room.

12. Modern control station.

13. Wheelsman on the Carferry Badger.

14. Deckhands pulling tarps on old style hatch covers.

15. Example of old hatch clamps, on tarped covers.

65

16. Telescoping hatch covers, need to be tarped.

17. Bos'n chair, the take-off.

18. Simple Bos'n chair.

19. Bos'n chair landing on the dock.

20. Deckhands washing down after loading cargo.

21. Engineer, Katrina Walheim

22. Katrina working in the engine room bilges.

23. Katrina next to propulsion diesel engine.

24. Katrina next to propeller, while in dry dock.

25. Three women engineers.

26. Chief Engineer Joyce Estelle in the engine room.

27. Chief Joyce in the Engineering Control Room.

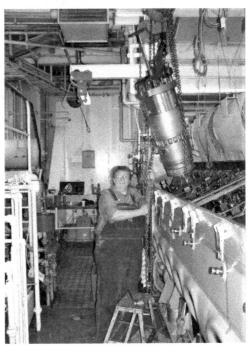

28. Chief Joyce next to propulsion engine.

CHAPTER 4

Why Are Men and Women Attracted to Sailing?

In the previous chapter, Kat Walheim mentioned the good paycheck. But many, if not most, young boys, particularly in the nineteenth and early twentieth centuries, were attracted to sailing because of the excitement. When people asked them what they wanted to be when they grew up, being a sailor was probably high on their list. Eventually, fireman, policeman, and cowboy were added to their list, but getting a job on a ship required minimal education and no prior training. Sailing appeared exciting and romantic, based upon the books and movies kids enjoyed in those days, and the money was better than similar jobs ashore.

The following story by Mike Braybrook describes this early fascination with ships. Some people move on to other things, but some never lose that attraction. See the old photos at the end of this chapter, showing the unloading of the Dutch ship he saw.

I grew up twenty miles inland from Muskegon, Michigan, where I first experienced lake boats and saltwater ships. As a youngster, I had an interest in ships, and my dad knew it. So, one day he heard about a Dutch ship coming to deliver a complete windmill, straight from Holland. After work one evening, he planned on going to Muskegon to visit a friend, and he asked me if I wanted to come along. He said we could see the Dutch ship while we were there, so of course, I wanted to go!

We drove to Muskegon, and he stopped to visit his friend, after which he and I drove down to the harbor, to the Mart Dock where the salties tied up.

After parking the car, we walked past the Milwaukee Clipper dock. The Clipper was somewhere out on Lake Michigan, on her way to Wisconsin. We walked on over to the guard shack at the gate to see if there was any way we could go down to see the salty. The gate was open, and there was no one in the guard shack. My dad looked around and didn't see anyone.

"What the heck, let's see how far we can get," he said with a wink. This surprised me, as he was usually one to go by the rules.

We went on through the gate and passed the large redbrick warehouse, then around a corner to an open area along the dock. And there she was! Not big by today's standards, but to this young, small-town lad, she was huge! By now it was early evening, so she had all her deck lights blazing. She had a light gray hull that was rust-streaked in places. Painted across the stern were the words Prins Willem. It was all very exotic to me, as I stood there soaking it all in.

She was a mid-1950s-built vessel, with the superstructure amidships, and a small deckhouse at the stern. I watched as a sailor came out of the deckhouse, and he quickly climbed a ladder to the top and started adjusting a TV antenna. Down below, someone hollered, telling him it was good now, so he climbed back down and then disappeared back into the deckhouse.

Other sailors and longshoremen were on the deck, hollering to each other over the din of the steam deck winches, which were pulling large wooden beams out of the holds. Those were *parts for the windmill, which was going to be reassembled in the town of Holland, down the coast.*

As I stood there, I could smell different odors coming off the ship, like the smell of fresh paint, manila rope, exhaust from the stack with a hint of warm oil. And I'm sure I got a whiff of something from the galley. It was heady stuff for a young fella who had an interest in anything to do with ships. It was exciting to see, smell, and experience something that I had only read about in books.

I could've stayed there all evening, watching the ship being unloaded, but Dad said we were pushing our luck, and might get "escorted out" at any time. So reluctantly we turned and headed back out the gate towards the car. As we went past the guard shack, there was still nobody home.

Sue Lieblein, a GLMA graduate who sailed the Great Lakes before going shoreside, now teaching at GLMA, offered a similar story:

The photo of Sue Lieblein at the end of this chapter was taken in 1994 when Sue became the first female chief engineer on the Great Lakes.

The husband of a friend of the family worked in the office of Pickands Mather, which used to be the parent company of Interlake Steamship. Apparently, in the old days, companies would give trips to each other, for employees and families to enjoy. My grandmother went on at least twenty trips with this man's wife.

I got a trip as a passenger when I was fourteen. I thought it was neat but wasn't interested in working in the galley so I didn't think much more about it until a few years later when I was in the Sea Explorers, and we had a guest speaker who worked for Cleveland-Cliffs. I asked if it was possible for women to get a job on the boats and to work their way up. That was the first time I had heard of the Great Lakes Maritime Academy.

I entered GLMA in the deck department, but during my sea project one season, I found the work in the engine room very interesting, so when I went back to school, I switched to the engineering department.

After I graduated from GLMA in 1986, there were no officer jobs available. Several of my engineer friends and I went to work on coastwise tankers, in unlicensed positions. We were wipers, oilers, and pumpmen. Then in 1987, sailing opened on the Lakes, and I started working for American Steamship.

The hard work and long hours either in a hot engine room or on cold weather decks never entered their minds. The potentially poor home life, being away from their family, was certainly never considered.

Many sailors were attracted by a life event, even after those childhood ideas. Mike Braybrook offers another story:

I call this a pre-sea story because it was before I went sailing for a career, and it was my first experience on the car ferry S.S. City of Milwaukee. It was 1967, and I was seventeen. My friend was eighteen, and we decided to take a motorcycle trip across the big lake [Lake Michigan] and see a little of Wisconsin. At the time, I lived in Casnovia, Michigan, which is inland from Muskegon. It was going to be a weekend trip, which would start after work on a Friday, so we didn't get to the dock till evening.

I had assumed that the Grand Trunk boats took vehicles as well as passengers, but we were in for a disappointment when we pulled into the dock and met the purser at the apron. When I asked to buy tickets for a trip, he informed us that they didn't take vehicles. We were bummed out and wondering what to do next. After a little thought, the purser said to hold on for a bit. He was going to go up and talk to the captain, and see what kind of mood he was in. He'd see what he could do for us.

A short while later, he came back with a smile and said, "Looks like you guys have lucked out tonight. We're gonna sneak your bikes aboard!"

The deckhands were more than happy to help manhandle the bikes onto the car deck, and tie them down, as it was somewhat of a novelty for them. The tickets were five dollars a head and $3.50 for a room and the bikes were free, as they "didn't exist." We were excited to watch the boat leave the dock and proceed out through the harbor. We went on past the lighthouse at the end of the piers, then out into the big lake. We wandered the decks and watched the lights of Muskegon fade into the distance.

Later, as we were walking by the crew's mess, the night cook stepped out on the deck for a smoke. We stopped to talk for a bit; he told us a little about the boat and his job, and then he said he had just set out the midnight lunch for the crew, who would be relieving the watch. He invited us in for a bite to eat, no charge. We were happy to oblige as we didn't even realize that we were indeed hungry! It was the first time I had seen beef tongue, which I didn't indulge in, and the first time that I had come across smoked chubs, which I did try and took a liking to.

After that, we decided to head to our cabin to get some sleep. My friend zonked out quickly, but I was still too excited to sleep, so I got back up, went out on deck, and enjoyed the warm summer's night breeze. I watched the lights of Milwaukee, which were starting to show on the horizon.

After daybreak, we pulled into the harbor and sailed to the Grand Trunk docks at the south end of the harbor. Our bike trip took us up the coast, where we made a stop so my buddy could get his first legal beer, as back then the legal drinking age was eighteen in Wisconsin. We made it to Manitowoc, where we took one of the C&O boats back to Michigan. I was intrigued by that nighttime boat trip, and I believe that it was partly responsible for my subsequent sailing career.

There are four photos at the end of this chapter, showing a new deckhand arriving at a ship for the first time. He is green and probably scared but trying to act like he knows the ropes. Unless his father, an uncle, or an older brother has sailed, this new man does not know what happens next. It is like entering boot camp in the military.

Luckily, the other crew members have probably been looking forward to this new guy's appearance because they were shorthanded. They will give him a hard time, maybe yell at him when he makes mistakes, but they will also teach him his job. Even new officer cadets out of the academies are entering a new world. They also have a trial by fire. But they learn fast. After one contract, they learn to love the job or they quit. The work is hard, but once they fit in with the rest of the crew, they start to feel at home.

Thank you to the Lake Carriers' Association for permission to use many of the photos at the end of this chapter, which were part of a training manual used for new hires.

A young man is dropped off at the gate of a loading facility. He tells the guard he has orders to board his ship. He shows the orders and is pointed down the dock, on a muddy road. There is equipment overhead and dirty ore dust—or coal—raining down on him. Many of these docks have a tunnel, as shown in one of those training photos, making it safer and cleaner to reach the ship. The entire experience is eerie and frightening for a new man heading to his first ship.

The young man now reaches the ship and the deck watch asks him who he is, and what he wants. He yells up over the machinery noise, saying he has orders to join the crew. The deck watch throws down a rope and hoists his luggage aboard, as shown in one photo.

The young man then climbs the long ladder. The Great Lakes ships seldom have a fancy, safe gangway, which is common on deep-sea ships.

He is finally aboard and directed to his room, which, on these older ships, is located in the forward deckhouse. He will change clothes and get right to work.

In various sections of this book, I will be including some great background and stories from retired Chief Engineer Bill Kulka. He ended his career as chief on the carferry *Badger*, running between Ludington, Michigan, and Manitowoc, Wisconsin. The *Badger*, by the way, is part of the U.S. Highway 10, even shown that way on official maps. Highway 10 stops and starts at the dock, in both Ludington and Manitowoc, and it says *U.S. Highway 10* on the sea gate—car-boarding door—on the stern of the *Badger*.

But back to Bill Kulka … Bill spent time in the Navy, which is very typical for a lot of sailors, including those on the Great Lakes. As Bill told me after his father died when he was in high school, his only "rich uncle" was Uncle Sam, so he joined the Navy. After boot camp, Bill went to Machinery Repairman Navy A School, where he became a machinist. He did well in that school and was assigned to the submarine base in Pearl Harbor. There, he gained a lot of hands-on experience with ship machinery. He quickly advanced to second-class petty officer and then made one cruise on an aircraft carrier.

Bill left the Navy and attended GLMA. However, Bill continued his Navy career as a reservist, spending much of his mandatory drill time working on Navy ships in Newport, Rhode Island. Bill retired as an officer in the Navy, reaching the O-5 level.

"I got interested in the Merchant Marine after meeting some guys off the U.S.N.S. *Nodaway*," Bill told me. "It was an old, tiny supply ship that went to Wake [Island], Midway [Island], and a lot of other little places I'd never heard of. When I got out of the Navy, I checked out Cal Maritime in Vallejo, California, but it was too much like the Navy. I had found out about GLMA in the [U.S.S. *Ranger*] carrier's library. The carrier's chief engineer, Commander Zimmerman, wrote a recommendation letter for me. The Academy wanted a letter from somebody in the shipping industry, and he qualified!"

Stories from Bill about his experience will be found in other chapters.

Although I was not a sailor, I had to deal with many of the same problems you'll read in this next story from Mike Braybrook, like going to one dock to find the ship had changed destinations. Nothing in the marine industry seems to be on a set schedule, with multiple changes making life interesting and sometimes crazy.

Here's a good story from Mike about his memories of his adventure trying to catch a ship:

Catching a boat to start a job isn't always the easiest thing to do. One time a dispatcher for Oglebay Norton called me for a relief job on the M.V. Wolverine. *I was supposed to catch it down in Holland, Michigan, in a couple of days. The following morning, he called me back and said he had to change my orders, now to catch the S.S.* Middletown *in Manitowoc. He thought that would be easy for me as I could just catch the ferry across the lake from Ludington. But then he paused, remembering it was November, and the ferry was laid up for the winter.*

"I'll find a way to get there," I said.

Later that afternoon he called back again, saying he had another change of orders, and that the Middletown *was now going to Marquette instead of Manitowoc. Well, now I had to find a way up to the Upper Peninsula and Marquette.*

The next morning, he called back once again and apologetically told me he had yet another change of orders, and the Middletown *was now going to Silver Bay, Minnesota!*

Well, I said, "She has to come back through the Soo, so I'll just catch her there." And he agreed. Oglebay Norton paid relief men up to five hundred dollars for travel expenses, so I took advantage of that. I booked a charter plane out of the local airport. The chief engineer on the Middletown *called me and gave me the approximate time the ship would be at the west approach into the MacArthur Lock, and I told the charter pilot what time I needed to be there.*

I lived right next to the Mason County Airport in Ludington, so I picked up my bags, went through a man gate in the fence, and walked across the airport property to the plane. The pilot packed my gear in the plane and handed me a newspaper, saying he'd have me at the Soo in a little over an hour. It was a short ten-minute ride from the Sault Ste. Marie Airport to the Soo Locks.

I went up to the guard shack and found three other guys standing there, also waiting for boats. Two were waiting for the Middletown, *and one for the upbound* Paul R. Tregurtha.

While we were waiting for transport down to the lock, we were asking where everybody was from. Come to find out, the conveyor man going to the Tregurtha *was from Scottville, just eight miles from where I lived! I asked how he got up here, and he said he drove his pickup and left it at the Soo warehouse. I jokingly told him that next time we should carpool!*

Another such story comes from one of the female engineers, Joyce Estelle, who spoke to me about why she decided on sailing as her career:

My folks had a cabin on the St. Mary's River [downstream from the Soo Locks] and we spent our summers up there. We all enjoyed watching the boats go by, and I remember thinking it would be cool to work on them, but it wasn't a realistic goal at the time. I was into sports in school and thought it would be neat to be a phys-ed teacher.

That career never got off the ground because my teaching certificate was too specialized. A friend gave me a birthday present about Great Lakes trivia, and there was an article about the Great Lakes Maritime Academy. That's where I learned that sailing was a possibility. My dad and my sister both asked if I was crazy—it still makes me laugh—but I went for it. It was a second career for me, as it was for Captain Lori Reinhart.

I grew up in northwest Ohio but currently live in Michigan, about a half hour east of Traverse City. I'm married with three cats and two dogs, and we enjoy living in the woods of northwest Michigan.

Joyce also gave me the following story about two fellow female sailors:

We don't know what got Denise started as a sailor, but Betty started sailing after her husband retired from sailing. Many sailing couples find it hard to see one another every day, once the sailor retires, so we wonder if that is what caused Betty to go to sea.

In addition to the women engineers and mates aboard ship, we have quite a few women stewards and second cooks on board. One of the photos at the end of his chapter shows Denise Chambers Fox on the left. She died from cancer back in 2013. Her sister, who was aboard as a guest/passenger, is next to her.

Denise was one of the feistiest people I've ever met: strong, confident, and hilarious. She always had a good rapport with everyone and knew who she could kid around with and did so often. She was a great shipmate, looking out for everybody. During the holidays, she did special things for all of us. We knew she was failing at the tail end of her final sailing season, but she never gave up. She never lost her sense of humor and gave her job 100 percent. We were all sad when she died.

The third lady is our second cook, Betty Benish, who retired two years ago. Betty worked for our company from December 2004 until the end of the 2018 sailing season.

Betty is one of the hardest-working gals I've ever met. She's about five foot nothing and was in her early seventies when she retired. She had more energy than most everyone here. When her husband, Richard, was sailing, she would pack the kids into the car and go visit him at the different ports throughout the Great Lakes, so they could see their dad. Back in those days, there was hardly any vacation at all, so wives commonly traveled to the various ports. Then when Richard retired, she went sailing, and he regularly came to visit us when we pulled into port. He would take a couple of trips with us each year.

AND WHY DO THEY KEEP GOING BACK?

I always wondered why people continued to go sailing each year. The work could be hard, sometimes dangerous. The pay was better than ashore, but most of the guys I knew were blowing their money on toys, booze, and some ladies before getting home. I had an uncle who sailed for a few years and each time he came home he had new cameras and fancy tools he'd never use, and any money he had left was gone before he went sailing the next spring. They were broke much of the time. Most of their marriages were failing.

My father was a little more responsible with his spending, but he had a movie camera in the early 1950s. I still own several of his cameras, projectors, and thousands of feet of 8mm film, which I recently donated to the Historical Collections of the Great Lakes in Bowling Green, Ohio.

The best way to explain why sailors went back is to ask the sailors themselves. So, here are comments from several Great Lakes sailors.

In Captain Lori Reinhart's words, this is why people decide to sail:

All those new sailors see is the nice paychecks, nice trucks, decent home for the family and kids, vacations, our "crazy" goals we're striving for. How it must be nice to have all these things, and not worry about anything like a "normal" person would.

What they don't see is when we pack our bags with tears in our eyes and our families' [eyes]. When we hug, kiss, and say goodbye to our loved ones. When they beg us not to go, but we still walk out the door. They don't see the miles we travel. They don't see the hours we work. They don't see the look on our faces when the closest thing to home is hearing about it through the phone. How our loved ones talk about their struggles, and we can't be there for them. I'm sure we've all at one point wanted to say "hell with this" and go back home. But there's a sacrifice to be made. We do it for them.

Here's to the brotherhood that makes that sacrifice. May we see the day that it pays off.

Captain Ed Wiltse sailed several times for extended periods but eventually went ashore. Here's his answer to the same question I asked Lori:

I know from my own circumstances why I got off the boats, and then returned to sailing three separate times in my career. I nearly did so again recently. Sailing offers relatively simple, honest work, excellent pay, and good benefits for the effort given, as compared to shore employment. It is a simple life, where troubles and concerns can be reduced to life on the ship.

The drawback is it is not a natural life. For most people, spending over half of one's days out at sea, away from loved ones, in a mostly industrial environment, with almost no ability for diversion, is a lot to take. It would be like working in a power plant or steel mill, but not being allowed to leave work for a month or two at a time. It can quickly become monotonous, soon after the newness wears off.

But when you can make two to three times the money per day sailing, compared to working ashore, many people feel they must stick with it. Some people become institutionalized after years of sailing. I knew several guys who would not get off the ship unless they were forced off, and then they just simply existed until they could come back to the ship. They seemed to lose the ability to connect with friends and loved ones and only felt comfortable on the ship.

I never wanted to be like that, which is why I came ashore rather than continue sailing. I guess that is why our friend John says, "Sailors and prostitutes get along so well because they understand each other." (I guess they both like the money, and they just can't quit.)

I always thought you would meet some of the most extreme characters out sailing— some of the best and some of the worst. Maybe living together on a ship just puts people under a spotlight, which they wouldn't otherwise be exposed to in a more normal shoreside existence.

I read a wonderful story written by a Great Lakes captain who retired after a career on the Great Lakes. He said I could use his words/sentiments, but he wished to remain anonymous. He praised his crew by name, telling stories about how they helped him, even bringing tea to his room on days he was sick, encouraging him to get to the bridge for arrival into some port.

That captain spoke about the loyalty of the sailors over the years, but also said that the new generation of sailors did not have the same dedication to their company or their job. He was retiring early because he was becoming disillusioned due to the quality of the new crew members coming aboard.

He felt a kinship with the old-timers, who were dedicated and hardworking. However, the new crop of young men coming aboard did not develop that loyalty. The captain felt that loyalty was necessary to do a good job, which he was used to in the past. They did not become part of the family-type cooperation, which made working with those old sailors so appealing.

And here, Mike Braybrook offers another story about a Great Lakes mariner who decided to take a contract aboard a deep-sea freighter. It gives some insight into the "up the street" escapades, which most sailors have had during their careers. Although this story took place off the Great Lakes, it is too good to ignore, and at least the sailor involved was normally a Great Lakes guy!

Another "recreation" story happened off the Lakes but it had its origins here. I sailed with a real character who was a fireman on the City of Midland. His name was Max. Once, he brought golf ball–sized clinkers from the boilers up on deck in a brightly painted box and sold them to passengers as official City of Midland paperweights. And yes, people bought them!

He was kind of a gypsy around the Lakes, constantly changing jobs, as he also sailed the Lakers as well as the tugboats. One winter when he was laid off, he decided to take a relief job out of a union hall on the West Coast. He shipped out on a Texaco tanker that was heading to Singapore. Once there, he went into the city and found a cozy bar to hang out in. While in the bar, a Russian Navy sailor wandered in. The Russian sailor spoke a fair amount of English, so he struck up a conversation with Max the fireman.

Max was wearing a ball cap with a U.S. Merchant Marine patch on it. The Russian said he wanted to buy that cap, but Max said it wasn't for sale. The Russian was pretty adamant that he wanted to buy the cap.

Well, Max devised a little scheme: he told the Russian they should drink shots until one of them passed out, and the winner would take both caps. Max suggested they drink vodka, and he was pretty sure the Russian would be happy with that. To get his scheme started, he went over to the barmaid and told her what they were going to do. On the sly, he gave her a sizable tip and told her to bring over a few shots at a time, making sure that his were filled with water.

It worked as planned, and he pretended to get drunk while the Russian did. Finally, the Russian's eyes rolled back in his head and he slid under the table. Max picked up his prize and beat feet back to his ship. A couple of months later, back aboard the Midland, he was telling me the story and said he hoped the sailor didn't get in too much trouble when he went back to his ship hatless.

There are some old photos at the end of this chapter, taken from my father's photo album. Many of the pictures showed the crew hamming it up for the camera. You could tell the crew enjoyed one another's company.

They lived together, ate together, and worked together twenty-four hours a day for months at a time. So it was more than the relationships you'd develop with fellow workers at a factory job. Those who did not fit in or who were not pulling their weight did not last long onboard a ship.

One of those photos at the end of this chapter shows the typical friendship between these crew members, standing next to the lifeboat. The man standing at the left, in the photo is my father. This clear camaraderie is a big reason why these men and women stay aboard for long, hard contracts away from family.

CAMARADERIE

Often, crew members developed great friendships. Some of these friendships spanned many years and some even continued beyond quitting the job or into retirement.

The following story from Mike Braybrook shows this friendship in the crew, as well as how sailors will do anything for a break. Getting off the ship to go "up the street" was an important break from the routine despite some hardships.

One of my more memorable shipmates on the car ferries was Lee from Oconto, Wisconsin. Lee was a boilerman on a Navy destroyer during WWII in the Pacific Theater. After mustering out of the Navy, he came back to the Lakes and sailed for the now-defunct Cleveland-Cliffs fleet. He took a job as a watertender on the C&O car ferries, because the Wisconsin ports they served were close to home. He would usually drive down to Kewaunee or Manitowoc to catch his boat when going back to work.

I was on the same watch with him aboard the City of Midland *for a couple of years, Lee working as a watertender and myself as oiler. We roomed together, and Lee could be amusingly predictable. When getting off watch, he would crawl into his bunk and say out loud, "Solid comfort," and then he would open a Zane Grey or Louis L'Amour paperback Western novel. When the coal passer would come around to wake us up for the next watch, clicking on the light, Lee would invariably say, "Daylight in the swamp!"*

Lee was a good shipmate to be around because he had a great sense of humor and was always upbeat. One time while we were underway during an evening watch, I was sitting on a tall stool by the starboard engine and Lee was sitting on a stool at the watertenders station, by the forward bulkhead. Andy, the second engineer, came over to talk and was lightly tugging on one of my shirt buttons. When it came off, the look on my face got to Lee, while Andy nonchalantly dropped the button into my pocket. Lee found it so hilarious that he started laughing hard enough to turn his face red and bring tears to his eyes! I've seldom seen anyone laugh that hard in my life.

It was January and we were heading to Manitowoc, Wisconsin. After watch, down in the flicker, we could hear the loose ice scraping along the hull as we entered the ice field outside the harbor.

We had just come off the 8–12 morning watch, and it was time for lunch. "We should go 'up the street' and drink our lunch," I jokingly said.

Lee paused, and said, "You know, I'm out of beer, and I could use one about now."

Well I had come up with the idea so I couldn't rightly back down now, so I said, "I'm game if you are."

We dressed warmly, as we knew it was cold outside, but we didn't know just how cold it was until we got up to the car deck. We were standing next to the mate, who was watching the deckhands secure the cables to the apron. He asked us if we were going uptown and if we knew it was only three degrees above zero with a stiff wind.

We looked at each other and neither of us wanted to be the one to wuss out, so we nodded in agreement that we were going. We walked off the boat, went past the ticket office, around the big coal piles, and up to Jay Street. When we turned the corner onto Jay, we were between the huge Budweiser grain silos and it was like walking into a wind tunnel! I don't think we went more than forty or fifty feet before we had to turn our backs to the wind, as the sharp cold was searing our faces. I had to keep looking over my shoulder to see where I was going and try not to trip over the snowdrifts.

We made it to the first bar a block and a half up the street. It was unfortunately closed. We guessed the owner figured no one would be going out for a drink in that weather. We walked another three blocks to Eighth Street and headed north two blocks to the river. Crossing the bridge, we were no longer protected from the wind by buildings so we caught the full brunt of it again.

By now, I was questioning my judgment regarding this little trip, but it was too late for that. We had to go two blocks beyond the river to the next bar, which was also closed. We made a right turn down a side street, where we knew there were two more bars, and finally, one was open! We went in and immediately peeled off our parkas, as they seemed to be permeated with cold air.

Looking at our half-frozen faces, the barkeep said we probably needed a shot of whiskey to thaw them out. We did not disagree! We settled in, enjoying the warmth of the place, and went through a couple of beers and some small talk with the barkeep and the only other patron there.

That time of year, there was no schedule for the boat, just unload, reload, and head back out, so we only had about an hour and a half before we had to be back. We both bought a six-pack of beer to go and pulled our gear back on. We trudged out the door, back into the stinging cold. We retraced our tracks and literally didn't see any other tracks in the snow.

We turned at Jay Street and stepped along lively with the wind now at our backs. When we got to the end of the street to make our turn, Lee stepped on some unseen ice underneath the snow. His feet went up in the air as he went down in a heap. As he struggled to his feet, he proudly held up his sack of beer, which never hit the ground! We hit it just right, arriving as they were getting ready to push the last string of railcars on the boat. Next would be the three or four autos that were making the trip. As we came across the stern and walked past the same mate, he just shook his head, probably wondering what the hell was wrong with our heads!

Some camaraderie does not require a trip up the street, as shown in this humorous story by Captain Aaron Menough. This occurred soon after an outing with Aaron's children to one of those restaurants where an entertainer was making balloon animals for the kids. Captain Menough thought it would be fun to make animals at home, so he bought a bag of those balloons and took them along on his next trip aboard his boat. He watched videos and practiced, wanting to amaze his kids the next time he was home.

With that as background for the story, the following is in Captain Menough's words:

I was up in the pilothouse, proud of my latest balloon sculpture. Behind me was my wheelsman, Pat. I enjoyed talking to him because he'd been sailing for so long. Pat was now in his sixties, and he had spent a lot of years working on Alaskan fishing and crab boats. He was a real man's man, from Freemont, Ohio. I'm from Toledo, so that made us neighbors. It was nice to have a connection with somebody from near my hometown.

I always explained to Pat what my kids meant to me, and he would always reciprocate my passion for my kids with all kinds of praise, then talk about his children, with a great sense of pride. Pat's daughter was still in high school, but a very bright straight-A student who was also on the swim team.

Pat's son was thirty-three, just four years younger than I was, and Pat mentioned he was in the Navy. Once again, I instantly related, as I had been in the Navy myself.

"My boy was active in the Navy SEALs," Pat said.

"That's amazing, Pat, go on," I said.

"Well it was something he always wanted to do, and he just did it."

"Just like that?" I said quite sarcastically. "Because who doesn't want to be a Navy SEAL?"

"He's a SEAL right now, this very moment?" I then asked, teasing him.

"No, right now he's finishing his PhD," replied Pat.

"Being a SEAL wasn't enough?" I said with a near sense of disbelief.

"The Navy is paying for him to do it, and he's doing it. Right now, he's a lieutenant commander, and he'll have his PhD this spring.

Feeling some sort of insecurity and personal discontent, I quickly changed the topic back to balloon animals.

"You know what, Captain Aaron? He's going to be at the dock tonight when we get to Toledo," said Pat.

"Oh cool, I want to meet him. Can I put him in a headlock?" I asked. And I don't know why I said that.

"Sure, if you want to. He has a good sense of humor," said Pat.

Normally, when people and crew members tell me they want me to meet their friends and family, I take it with a grain of salt. The boat schedule changes, or people can't find their way to the dock, or it just gets too late so nobody feels like coming down. I hear this all the time. With Pat's son flying in from San Diego, the odds were slim to none he would make it down to the Toledo coal dock on a Friday night.

We arrived at the dock just after midnight. It was an easy night for me. I made the dock with no difficulty and promptly went back to bed. I must've been asleep for forty-five minutes when my intercom rang.

"Ya?" I said in a sleepy haze. There was no response, just a pause.

A second buzz on the intercom, longer than the first, most certainly got my attention.

"Ya?!" I shouted.

"Hey, Cap, are you up? I'd like you to meet my son."

I was now wide awake and aware of Pat's old man voice. "Holy Jesus," I thought to myself. "The SEAL?" It suddenly became real.

I fumbled around in the dark, and already in an old pair of sweatpants, I grabbed the first shirt I could find and threw it on. I stepped out into the hallway and Pat was standing next to a man who I thought was James Bond for a moment. Pat's son was a very handsome, well-dressed, fit-looking man. Next to him was a stunning blonde woman. It was two thirty in the morning. Not only was Pat's son well educated but also well versed in navigating his way around Toledo at two in the morning.

I must admit that talking with Pat earlier in the pilothouse about his son's accomplishments made me feel like I had maybe wasted some of my youth. Over the next two minutes, that feeling would be solidified.

I thanked him for coming out to the boat and told him I was glad he could make it. I mentioned something about him finishing his degree, trying to muster up some conversation.

"Yes, this spring, from Florida," he replied.

"Wow, Florida. Goooo Gators or whatever appropriate dwelling mascot creature," I said, and then silently reflected on how poorly I did in school. I was able to form those words, and then I looked down and realized I was wearing a T-shirt that said Big Daddy across the front, in four-inch bold letters.

I could sense the self-induced shame building over my head. "So, you were in the Navy too, your dad mentioned?" I asked. "Yes, I was a SEAL, but I'm not active in that now," he replied very humbly.

"Valedictorian of his high school class and he excelled in football and baseball. But the Navy wanted him to play football exclusively," Pat then piped in.

"Well," Pat's son said, "I just wanted to focus on my academics."

"Of course," I said, lying in two words and flippantly laughing to imply I knew what he was going through. In reality, I was the person who was shuffled off to technical school with the potheads and grease monkeys just to have a chance of graduating. "You got to focus on those academics," I said, all snide and sarcastic.

My self-esteem and confidence now set to "stun," I didn't feel like looking anybody in the eye. Keeping my eyes on the floor, I then also noticed, quite un-James Bond–like, that there were holes in my slippers.

Clearly making an impression parallel to a train-riding hobo, I pushed what was left of my bedhead hair aside and said, "I can make a dinosaur out of balloons." Again, I have no idea why.

My five-year-old voice emerged quite politely. "Would you like one? It'll just take a minute."

"Umm, no, thanks, that's okay. We've had a long flight, and we're going to head home," Pat's son said.

His eyes and the woman's beautiful inconvenienced stance were enough to say, Are you sure this guy is the ship's captain, Dad?

"I have a whole bag of balloons."

That phrase came out of my adult body like a ventriloquist voice through a dummy.

Having done enough damage for one conversation, we parted ways, and I went back into my room. I sat in my chair and wondered about what just happened for a moment, thinking, Could I even fill out a university application?

I reflected quietly for a few moments and did what any grown man would do: I took a deep breath, inflated my next balloon, and started sculpting a sword. I probably would've stuck it through my chest, had it been real.

I think we've all had moments like that, wishing we could go back and start a conversation all over again. You want to make a good impression, and everything goes wrong.

TATTOOS

You will glean from many of the pictures in this book, that sailors tend to like tattoos. This is universal, for those on the Great Lakes and deep sea. Although many tattoos are from previous military service, some are Merchant Marine related. Just like the pride in the military, most Merchant Mariners are also proud of their jobs. Most are very loyal to their companies, particularly on the Great Lakes, and they tend to sail for the same company for many years, if not their entire career.

Tattoos are a way of showing their dedication and pride.

Mike Braybrook and I are two such examples. The tattoos shown in photos at the end of this chapter show Mike Braybrook's merchant marine tattoos , and also my U.S.C.G tattoo. Neither are as fancy as the other example, but they were probably much cheaper!

SO HOW ARE WOMEN ACCEPTED ON BOARD?

Women have been part of the Great Lakes marine industry for many years. In many cases, they have been the owners of tugboat companies, like Selvick Marine Towing in Sturgeon Bay, which was owned by two sisters. That company is now owned by another woman, Julie Sarter. There was also Holly, owner of Holly Marine Towing in Chicago.

Deep-sea sailors always said that women were bad luck aboard a vessel, but women started sailing as cooks and stewards in the galleys of Great Lakes cargo ships in the early twentieth century. The car ferries also started using female crew for housekeeping duties, food service, and hospitality roles in the early twentieth century.

The physical aspect of the start-up position in the marine crews made it difficult for women. The entry-level deck crew job was deckhand, which involved pulling hatch cover tarps, pulling heavy mooring cables, and lots of shoveling of spilled cargo. The entry-level engine crew job was coal passer or fireman, which also required physical strength.

Not that some women didn't try—and succeed—in those start-up positions, but they were not cut any slack because of their sex. Some were injured as a result. Mike Braybrook remembered one female coal passer who injured her wrists by wielding a forty-pound ash hoe in the boiler room. Many men wash out in those jobs as well, but physical size and strength can certainly hurt a woman's chances to succeed in those jobs.

Quarters were also a problem in those old days. The deck crew and entry-level engine crew slept two, even four to a room, with no privacy. Restrooms were always shared back then, though that has changed today.

As previously stated, in the 1970s, possibly as a result of the Vietnam War, there was a need for additional maritime officers, and more women started to attend Merchant Marine academies, such as the one located in Traverse City. Many of the graduates from the East Coast and West Coast academies, including the U.S. Merchant Marine Academy, also started applying to Great Lakes shipping companies.

The result was that women started sailing on the Great Lakes as mates and engineering officers. Those who stayed became captains and chief engineers. Officers generally had a private cabin and their own toilet and shower, except on the old ships.

MISSING THE BOAT

This next story from Mike Braybrook describes not only the cama-raderie between the crew members but also the respect they receive from people on shore, both those they work with and others they meet:

> It's inevitable that at some point if you've sailed long enough, you're going to miss the boat. If it's on a Laker, you're going to have a problem getting to the next port the boat is headed for. On a car ferry, it's not as bad because you can catch it on the return trip. Usually!
>
> I was sailing on the City of Midland, and it was late September. We were no longer on scheduled trips, which was called running wild, heading to whatever port had the next load of freight. We were coming into Milwaukee, and Bobby and I decided to go "up the street" for a beer. The mooring slip on Jones Island is a good mile from the nearest bar, so we started walking as soon as the boat tied up. Arriving at the bar, we settled in and ordered a beer. We knew we wouldn't have a lot of time, so we only had one and grabbed a six-pack to go.

Walking the long stretch of road down Jones Island, we were still almost a quarter mile from the boat when I heard her whistle start blowing. We thought it was the beginning of the twenty-minute call, but it was only one short blast, which meant she was pulling out of the slip! What we didn't know beforehand was after the boat was unloaded, there was only a short load going back. It was an "oh crap" moment!

Well, we just kept walking toward the dock while we watched the boat pull away, wondering what we were going to do. When we got to the ticket office, we sat down on a bench and cracked a beer open, while we figured out a solution. Normally the boat would go to Manitowoc or Kewaunee after leaving Ludington, so we had to figure out how to get up there. There was one little problem: we had about twelve dollars between us, and back then, neither of us had a credit card.

While we were pondering our predicament, a railroad switchman walked up and stopped. He said, "Well, well, it looks like a couple of fellas missed the boat!"

Then he said it was our lucky day because the boat was coming back to Milwaukee next trip, and he couldn't just leave us stranded there overnight. After he finished switching out the railcars, he would come around and pick us up in his car. We thought that was decent of him because we barely knew him. We had only said hi on a few occasions in passing.

Once we got to his place, he said to sit down at the kitchen table while he went to get his dog, and he'd bring him in to meet us. When he brought in the dog, I could see why he wanted us to sit quietly at the table. The dog was menacing-looking, an all-black German shepherd named Killer. After he sniffed around us for a bit, we were deemed to be okay.

By now it was late afternoon, and Ron, the switchman, said we should go out on the town to celebrate missing the boat. We had left the boat wearing our work clothes. They were clean, but they were still work clothes. Ron said he couldn't take us out on the town looking like that, so he dug out a couple of sport shirts for us to change into.

After a bit, we headed out to the first bar. Anyone familiar with Wisconsin knows there is a neighborhood bar on almost every other corner. Having so little money, we were prepared to nurse our drinks all evening. That ended up not being a problem.

It seemed like Ron knew a lot of the people in every bar we hit. The first thing he would say when we all bellied up to the bar was, "Hey everybody, want you to meet a couple of sailors I know who missed their boat!"

After that, our money was no good, and there was always someone who wanted to buy us a beer.

Eventually, the night came to an end, and we went back to Ron's house, where he found us a place to sleep it off. The next morning, he supplied us with copious amounts of coffee to bring us back to the land of the living. Ron had to get us back to the dock early because he had to switch out the newly arrived train long before the boat came in. We ended up on the same bench we were on the afternoon before.

We were both feeling the effects of a dandy hangover coming on, and I think we both had the same idea when we saw a small ferry coming across the harbor. It was bringing employees of the city's Milorganite plant to work, and we thought maybe we might catch a ride back across, find a bar to hang out in, and wait for our boat to arrive. We thought a little hair of the dog might help us through our misery.

When the boat finally made her appearance, we took the ferry back across the harbor and walked onto the car deck. We were a bit sheepish and ready to face the music.

When I read they were taking the little ferry across the harbor for the "hair of the dog," I thought they were going to miss their boat for a second time!

1. Dutch ship which caught Mike Braybrook's attention.

2. This experience led to Mike becoming a sailor.

3. Sue Liellein, first woman Chief Engineer in U.S. fleet.

4. New hire, finding his way to the ship, through dock tunnel.

5. New hire going up the ship's ladder.

6. New hire sending his bags up to the ship via a rope.

7. New hire heading forward to his room.

8. Women cooks on Great Lakes freighter with friend visitor.

9. Happy, but dirty engineroom crew.

10. Author's father, Matt Ojala, on the S.S Harry Yates.

11. Hamming it up for the camera; author's father at left.

12. Tattoos are popular with many sailors. 13. Mike Braybrook's tattoos.

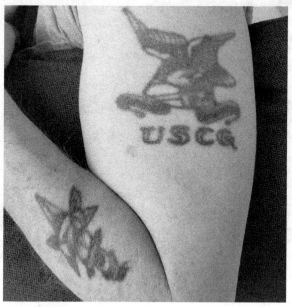

14. The author's tattoos.

CHAPTER 5

Food and Free Time

T he food on most Great Lakes ships was fantastic, and still is on many of the lake freighters. Some companies have gone to pre-packaged meals, to reduce the galley staff, but the crew does not appreciate this. The old saying about the Army traveling on their stomachs certainly applied to the mariners on the ships I saw, and those I worked on over the years.

In 1966, I had just been discharged from the Coast Guard and was working at Fort Howard Paper Company in Green Bay, Wisconsin. My father's ship at the time arrived in Green Bay to discharge cargo, and I went to his ship for a visit. We were going to have dinner aboard: some beautiful T-bone steaks. Except for my father and those standing watch, the ship was nearly empty. Most of the crew had gone "up the street" for a few beers and some bar food.

During dinner, the steward came into the dining room and asked if I could make use of some steaks. He had cooked up quite a few, expecting the crew to be aboard. The steward said most of the guys would come back having already eaten at the bar, so he knew the steaks would go to waste. He said he would save enough for the late shift night meals but asked me to take six nice T-bones home. I ate well for lunch at work for over a week.

Holidays aboard Great Lakes ships were a real gastronomical experience. I remember my father telling us about those meals for

105

Thanksgiving, Christmas, Easter if they were sailing late or early, and even the Fourth of July. The cooks and stewards were given a huge budget by the shipping company to put on a real feast. It was not just limited to food, but extra gifts for the crew, such as cigars and cigarettes, candy, and so on.

The next story is from Mike Braybrook and took place during one of his cargo-ship sailing years. The story describes the great Thanksgiving meal but also how rough weather can cause problems:

In 1981, I was working as a stoker aboard the venerable old steamer the Irvin L. Clymer. *We were heading eastbound toward the Straits of Mackinac. It was Thanksgiving Day, and I was looking forward to the feast, which I knew the galley crew was putting out.*

There was a strong wind coming out of the west, with whitecaps as far as the eye could see. The waves were getting higher as they were building through the restriction caused by the narrow Straits of Mackinac. I had the 12-4 watch, and I decided to get to the galley earlier than usual because I wanted some extra time to partake in the big meal at hand.

From my porthole, I watched as the Mackinac Bridge went overhead as the boat sailed under it. The boat was empty, so it was riding high in the water, and she was pitching more because of it. We were heading to Port Dolomite to take on a cargo of limestone. I went from my room in the doghouse, located on the deck above the mess room, and entered the door just forward of the galley. There I met an AB with the same idea I had, to get an early start on the Thanksgiving meal. We went into the crew's mess and asked the porter if they were serving yet. He asked the steward and got the OK to take our orders.

As always for a holiday meal on a Laker, it was hard to decide what to pick off the extensive menu, but we both managed to choose, and the porter went off to fill our orders. Each place setting had extra goodies around it for you to take with you after your meal. These included cans of mixed nuts, boxes of chocolates, bags of hard candy, sodas, assorted flavors of gum, packs of cigarettes, and a couple of cigars. There was so much extra stuff on the table, the galley crew had put a colorfully wrapped board supported on two big cans down the middle of the table with more goodies on it.

I stuffed myself but tried to leave enough room for dessert. Of all the desserts on the menu, the one I had never experienced was baked Alaska. So, I decided [to try it]. As the porter was bringing it in, I heard the phone ring in the galley. I saw the steward/first cook go over to answer it, and about the same time, I could sense the boat starting to come around to port. I then saw the steward angrily take his cap off, throw it to the deck, and stomp off into the pantry.

The captain had called down to tell him we were going to change course and haul around to head towards Port Dolomite. The steward was upset because he didn't get a heads up until the last minute, and he couldn't do much for what was about to happen. As the boat slowly came around, she was broadside to the high waves for a bit, and the boat started to roll badly. Things on our table and out in the galley started to slide back and forth and, ultimately, crash to the deck. The AB and I both reached for the plank in an attempt to save it from going over. We did save the plank, but of course, everything on it went sliding off. Out in the galley, the crab bisque, chicken soup, and turkey giblet gravy, all on top of the range, dumped over onto the deck. The range doors slammed open, and I saw two turkeys fly out and head toward the open galley door as if they were in a race.

There was quite a racket as everything else loose in the galley crashed to the deck. As the boat slowly came around and quit rolling, things quieted down again. We were both a bit late to relieve the watch by then, so we got up and started wading through all the dishes and Thanksgiving trappings lying about on the deck. Being a cigar smoker, I picked up a few that were mixed with all the wreckage with one hand while carrying my baked Alaska with the other.

The galley crew had eaten earlier, and other than the AB and me, nobody else in the crew got to eat Thanksgiving dinner that day. They were able to salvage enough to put together a decent meal for the crew that evening. One of the porters told me that was the only time he ever had to clean out the galley with a shovel!

And I did grab a menu knowing they wouldn't need it anymore.

The photos at the end of the chapter shows the menu from the meal described above, and also an example of a much fancier holiday menu. The original would have been in color, with a photo of the ship at the upper left.

One of the pictures at the end of the chapter also shows a typical setting of the everyday table in the crew's mess.

Another picture from the Lake Carriers' Association, shows a steward serving dessert, and another photo shows the crew mess on the *Joseph L. Block*, set up for a Holiday meal.

It seems like Thanksgiving is a great time to be aboard ship, based upon all the great meals described, but then again, it is November. November is notorious as the worst month on the Great Lakes. Many stories (the *Fitzgerald*, *Morrell*, and *Bradley* sinkings) occurred in November.

Two photos from Captain Lori Reinhart show a Christmas party aboard her last ship. ·

I checked my father's discharge book, and in thirty-two years of sailing, he ate twenty-eight Thanksgiving dinners and four Christmas dinners aboard ship.

Here is another story from Captain Wiltse about his Thanksgiving dinner experience:

I remember Thanksgiving Day on the Armco *back in 1987. By this time, I was sailing as a mate on board, and we were headed upbound, in ballast on Lake Superior. The weather that day was cold and gray, with a brisk west wind blowing. The ship was pounding into the head seas but was riding well and not moving too much.*

After finishing my noon watch, I returned to my stateroom to put on a sweater in the spirit of the holiday and stepped out on the spar deck to head back aft to the galley.

The galley crew prepared a tremendous holiday meal that day. Three people worked full time in the galley on the Lakers back in those days. The menu offered a full turkey dinner with all the trimmings, lobster tail with drawn butter, and New York strip steaks grilled to order with a baked potato.

Being relatively young—I was in my early twenties back then—with a correspondingly high metabolism rate, I thought it was a matter of pride to see how much I could digest in one sitting. So, not wanting to miss out on any of the special entrees on the menu that day, I decided to have them all. The meal was splendid, and I enjoyed it fully, all three entrees and sides, right through to dessert.

After a thoroughly enjoyable meal, along with some relaxing conversation with my shipmates around the dining table, it was time to head back forward up to my room for a nice nap. I stepped out onto the spar deck and felt the slap of the bitter Lake Superior west wind sting my face. I leaned into the wind while working my way forward along the starboard side.

About the time I got to about hatch five, I started to get lightheaded and dizzy. I am not sure if it was the cold brisk wind or the huge meal I ate, or both. I had to stop and sit down on the hatch for a bit to collect myself. After a few minutes, I started forward again and made it up to my nice warm stateroom, where I flopped down on the bunk and had a nice long nap.

As I drifted off to sleep, my heart seemed to struggle to push the blood around my sluggish body, stuffed with such a huge, fantastic meal. But oh, what a good feeling it was on that cold Thanksgiving night, out on Lake Superior. I can still remember that day, thirty-two years ago, like it was yesterday.

There are some photographs at the end of this chapter showing crew members *not* getting dirty. This camaraderie is one of the reasons many crew members return each year. One shows an accordion player crew member on the car ferry the Badger, and another shows two crew members eating a leisurely lunch outside the galley, aboard the car ferry Badger."

Occasionally, there are instances where the cook is not well liked. I should say, their food is not well liked. The next story by Captain Aaron Menough shows that the crew still cared about the cook's feelings, even though they hated her cooking:

Not all the animals are stowaways, like in some other stories I will tell. For example, Port Inland used to have a fox that lived near the edge of the dock and would come out to the boats every time we loaded. At first, we thought it was fascinating to watch the little red furball approach the side of the vessel, taking our leftover bread. However, he became useful when we would get our worst cooks aboard.

We had a cook who got upset when nobody would eat her food. Yet each morning, all the peanut butter was gone and three loaves of bread had been consumed as well as miscellaneous cereal boxes devoured. People would eat peanut butter for weeks, just to avoid her food. Finally, we wised up. To dodge any more incidental hurt feelings, we started throwing her entrees over the rail to feed the fox every time we went to Port Inland. I figured everybody was a winner. The cook thought people were eating her food, and the fox was leaving with a distended stomach.

This arrangement worked out great until one day, as we were leaving the dock, the cook was standing at the railing talking to another crew member. The boat skidded down the 600-foot length of the dock, and when the galley went by the fox hole she said, "That's where the fox lives, right?"

"Yes," I said. "He pops his head out of that little corner there," I continued, pointing in the proper direction.

"That looks like a stack of bones next to his hole!" she said.

My palms started to sweat at the sight of the leftover chicken dinner. I wasn't sure if she was astute enough to put our criminal crew members together with those bones.

"Just coincidence I'm sure," I said.

I pretended the captain was calling me by putting my hand up to my shoulder and faking a radio call. Then I slowly began to tiptoe backwards, desperate to avoid any confrontation. I noticed everyone else in the area doing the same.

"Hey! Goddammit!" she said. "Those are my mashed potatoes!" And she stomped off to her room.

"Well, this really stinks," I said. "It looks like we are going to have to start eating her food again or throw it overboard late at night."

"Well, don't feel too bad," said Wally, our engineer. "The fox wouldn't eat it, either."

FREE-TIME ACTIVITIES

When not on watch, sailors tend to have a lot of free time. When in port, they run "up the street" for a couple of quick drinks, as mentioned before. When aboard, they sometimes have hobbies. They play cards and occasionally gamble, and today's sailors have computers or electronic games on board.

One of my uncles sailed for a few years, and he was a great machinist. He built working models of old triple-expansion, reciprocating steam engines. He would hook them up to compressed air, and they worked. He also took up wood carving, and after retirement, he became quite an artist, displaying his pieces at shows.

Mike Braybrook describes some of these leisure-time activities:

The standard watch on most ships is four hours long, and then you have eight hours off. Then you stand another four-hour watch, with another eight hours off, completing your twenty-four-hour day. One of those eight-hour stretches is typically used to sleep, and the other is used for everything else you need to do: chores, maybe laundry, and recreation.

On the car ferries, which are in port several times a day, you could head home for a couple of hours if you lived near one of the ports. Otherwise, you would take that opportunity to go "up the street."

Recreation on the boat could be anything that can be done aboard a steamship. Back in the day, card playing was big; poker and cribbage got top billing. Getting off watch and having a few drinks with other guys off watch was popular. (Even though alcohol was never approved for use onboard, drinking in small amounts was ignored, up until the mid-1980s. That was when the Coast Guard cracked down on drinking.)

There were always hobbies like leatherworking, stamp collecting, knife making, and even furniture refinishing. Reading was also a popular pastime. A few guys would have full bookshelves in their rooms and would swap books with other readers. There were piles of magazines and newspapers in the rec rooms to choose from.

We had a chief engineer who would bring old bicycles aboard and rebuild and repaint them. Some he would give away, and others would stay on the boat for the crew to ride "up the street." We had another guy who loved to cook, and he had a mini kitchen set up in his room. He made a lot of his own meals. When you came down into the flicker you always knew when he was cooking!

In recent years, as younger guys have started to sail, they have brought more electronics aboard, like computers and video games. Companies are now expected to provide satellite TV and internet, so the younger crew tend to seclude themselves in their rooms. So the card games and drinking parties have all but disappeared.

One of my favorite recreation stories from back in the day was when a shipmate found an old cap-and-ball black-powder revolver at a yard sale. He brought it back to the boat and proceeded to clean the rust off and get it usable again. He got a hold of some black powder and round lead balls and decided the main coal bunker was a good place to try it out. He took a solid oak block of wood, about five inches thick, to use as a target. Neither of us knew much about black-powder firearms, so it was a surprise when he shot at the wood block, expecting the ball to penetrate it. But instead, it ricocheted back between our heads and hit the steel bulkhead right behind us! We decided that shooting inside the boat was probably not a good idea!

On the Great Lakes, many crew members stayed on the same ship for years. Chuck Cart's next story shows how crew members become family:

Being like "family," pranks amongst the crew were common, and we had a wiper who was the subject of some of them.

On one trip to Bath, Ontario, we had drained the starboard potable water tank to recoat it. Since we were a cement carrier, the age-old recipe for the potable water tank coating was as follows: put four gallons of clean water in a five-gallon pail, add enough Portland cement to make a paint-like consistency and a can of beer to kill the alkaline taste of the mixture. The chief said it would take six buckets to coat the tank and gave us six cans of beer for the job. Not all the beer made it into the mix. Spillage, you understand …

After we coated the tank, we went up on deck for some fresh air and noticed that the kids near the dock were catching some fish. We asked them to put a couple in an empty coffee can we had, and we put this near the manhole to the tank where we had left the tools for the wiper to clean and put away. Pretty soon, here he came with the can of fish and asked where they had come from. So we explained there must be a hole in the seawater suction screen because they were in the drinking water. We then told him that was why we had to clean the tank.

The wiper went all around the ship telling the crew not to drink the water because it had fish swimming in it. The manhole cover was usually stenciled in blue letters FRESH WATER, *and that night on watch, I repainted it to read* FISH WATER. *Last time I saw it, it was still stenciled that way!*

There are four photos at the end of this chapter from Jim Fay's 1937 collection. The first two show a ship's crew playing baseball in an empty cargo hold.· Crew members find a lot of ways to at least try to lead a normal life. Baseball was not a normal pastime, but playing cards was nearly a daily pastime, as shown in one photo. Most games were for money, but usually nickel limit.

Of course, the crew needed to look sharp for those ventures "up the street." They never knew when they might meet the girl of their dreams!

There was always someone aboard with some talent as a barber, but judging from some haircuts I've seen over the years, their experience was questionable.

One of the more talented guys I've heard about who made good use of his spare time was a man named Richard Soli. He sailed as third assistant engineer aboard the car ferry the *City of Midland*. He liked to paint during his time off watch, and there are two photos at the end of the chapter showing a sample of his work. Richard died, but after he retired he gave those two paintings, showing the carferries in dock, to Mike Braybrook. I'm sure Richard never thought of a career as an artist, but I've seen much worse hanging in art studios.

1. Typical Holiday dinner table onboard.

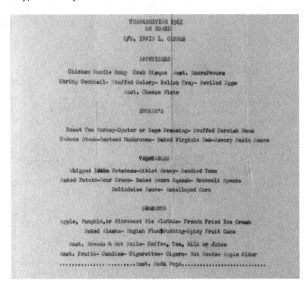

2. Typical old shipboard Holiday menu.

Menu

Appetizers
Shrimp Cocktail / cocktail sauce
Stuffed Celery
Deviled Eggs
Cheese Ball w/ Party Crackers

Soup Du Jour
French Onion Soup

Entrée's
Lobster Tail w/ Drawn Butter
Broiled Filet Mignon
Wine Mushroom Sauce
Baked Roast Chicken
Chicken Stuffing Dressing
Chicken Gravy

Vegetables
Baked Potato w/ Sour Cream
Sweet Green Peas
Steamed Green Asparagus

Pies
Apple, Cherry, Pumpkin, Mincemeat
Alamode

Extras
Chips, Pretzels, Nuts, Chocolates, Candy, Gum

Beverages
Apple Cider, Assorted Soda, Egg Nog, Coffee

3. Modern day Holiday menu.

4. Normal crew's mess table.

5. Galley Porter setting the table for dinner.

6. M/V Joseph Block's Holiday table.

7. Christmas celebration aboard ship.

8. Christmas gifts for the crew is typical on most ships.

9. Crewman playing accordion on the Carferry Badger.

10. Crewmen eating lunch on the Carferry Badger.

11. Friendly Cook and Porter on the Carferry Badger.

12. Playing baseball in the cargo hold of a Great Lakes ore carrier.

13. Batter Up; in the cargo hold.

14. Playing cards is a typical pastime for crew members.

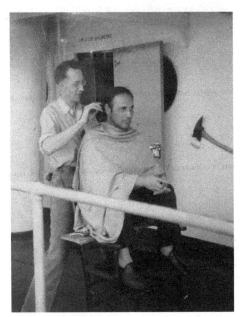

15. No time for haircuts ashore, so somebody always volunteers.

16. Some crew members are excellent artists.

17. This artist's paintings are as good as photos.

CHAPTER 6

Living Conditions

The crew's rooms on most Great Lakes ships, particularly the older ones, were generally better than the deep-sea ships of the same era. Great Lakes shipowners wanted to make money, but they seemed to understand they needed to keep good crew. Just like the good food described previously, the rooms were comfortable, except for the lack of air-conditioning. Crew rooms were small on the older ships but not cold and damp like those on the ocean tramp freighters. Newer ships are well decorated and comfortable but don't have the classic looks of the older ship's rooms.

There are several photos at the end of this chapter showing some typical berthing areas for Great Lakes ships. The first photo is typical for junior officers in the car ferry flicker.

There are two photos showing typical quarters on the older Lakers, including ore carriers and cement carriers, built in the 1920s to 1950s. I remember that decor from the boats I visited when my father was sailing.

Then there are two photos showing typical decor of the more modern vessels, built in the 1970s and afterwards. Although they look comfortable, the older vessels had a lot more to offer, such as the built-in desks and dressers. However, the new ships are typically air-conditioned.

1. Stateroom in the 'flicker' for engineers on carferries.

2. Typical old-style bunkroom on Great Lakes freighter

3. Typical bunkroom furniture on old freighters.

4. Typical modern bunkroom on Great Lakes freighter.

5. Typical bunkroom furniture on modern freighters.

CHAPTER 7

Unusual Great Lakes Vessels

MAIL BOATS

B efore the "sixty days on, thirty days off" contracts, it was tough for sailors to maintain relationships with their loved ones. It may have been even tougher for the families. Many ships were running iron ore and other bulk cargoes from Lake Superior to the steel mills in Ohio, so passing Detroit on the Detroit River was a regular occurrence.

As a child, I remember my mother having me write letters to my father and then inserting a picture or two into the envelope—maybe with a child's drawing, as well—and addressing the envelope as follows:

MATT OJALA
S.S. *HARRY YATES*
C/O WESTCOTT COMPANY
DETROIT, MICHIGAN

Today, the address is the same, except you must add a zip code. In the case of the above example, it would read *ZIP CODE 48222*. This zip code actually belongs only to the mail boat, which is very unusual.

There is one old picture at the end of this chapter, taken by Matt Ojala, showing the Westcott mail boat in the Detroit River, circa 1950. It had just delivered mail to his ship.

There is also a picture from a postcard, showing the *Westcott II* with the bridge between Detroit and Windsor, Ontario, in the background.

BUMBOATS

I remember being on several bumboats with my father in the Toledo and Duluth harbors. The *Marine Trader* in Duluth was outfitted with shelving for displays and coolers for the beer. It carried everything the sailors asked for, and if they didn't have something, they promised to stock it before the next trip. If a sailor wanted something special or unusual, the bumboat would order it for him and have it by their next trip, even gifts for wives and girlfriends.

The bumboats also took outgoing mail and would deliver mail if it was sent to them, but this was not their main function. A bumboat was more or less a floating convenience store, and sometimes a few crew members would congregate aboard to have a couple of beers, but generally, you went aboard to do your shopping for cigarettes, snacks, film, batteries, and maybe a birthday card to send home.

These boats were a common sight in many Great Lakes ports, though some larger East Coast ports had similar operations. Such boats still operate in places like Singapore, but bumboats are mostly a thing of the past.

Kaner Brothers (Bumboats)–Superior

The following information was graciously provided from the Kaner Brothers family website. Allan Garon allowed the use of this information: One of the photos at the end of this chapter is a reproduction of an old newspaper article, giving some history of the Duluth bum boat company. The Kaner Brothers owned and operated the service boats that sold supplies to the ships that came to the Duluth-Superior port. They were called bumboats. An early boat was named the *Kaner II*.

The *Marine Trader* was launched in 1939 and was owned and operated by Alan Charles Kaner (from 1942-1986).

Sue Lieblein told us she only had one chance to experience a bumboat, which was one of the Kaner-owned boats. She said it was in 1985 in Superior, and the chief took her down to have a few beers. She said she never went back.

I found another picture of a bumboat on Facebook and the owner of the picture, Bob Haworth, another Great Lakes ore boat sailor, graciously allowed its use in this book. That photo shows a Kaner bumboat moored alongside an ore boat, loading cargo in Duluth/Superior harbor.

It was a sad day when the bumboats disappeared, but the numerous convenience stores, many located near enough to the harbors, made the bumboats relatively expensive. The shorter contracts also meant the sailors could take enough supplies along from home so that frequent replenishment during a contract was not necessary.

Mike Braybrook shared this memory of his experience onboard a bumboat:

I had heard about the bumboats that serviced vessels on the Lakes, and I finally got to see one while on my first Laker. I picked up the job in early November, and the second trip we made was to Toledo, for a cargo of coal. As we pulled into the Sputnik dock, I asked one of the deck gang if the bumboat was still in operation this late in the season. He said he was sure it wasn't.

I looked out across the harbor and didn't see it coming, so I figured he was right. A couple of days earlier, I was offered a beer—or three—and I wanted to reciprocate, so I decided to take a cab into town to pick up some beer, along with a few other odds and ends. I went down the accommodation ladder and crossed the dock to a pay phone to call a cab. While on the phone, I noticed a young fella with longish hair walking along the deck and I didn't recognize him as being in our crew, so I figured he must've been part of the dock crew.

I took the cab into town for my supplies, and when I returned, I saw the bumboat had come alongside and was just leaving. They moved down the dock to tie up alongside a Canadian boat, just ahead of us. It turned out the fella I saw with the longish hair, walking up the deck, had come off the bumboat and was going around our lake boat letting the crew know they were alongside.

I wanted to get on that bumboat to see what they had to offer, so I walked down the dock to the Canadian boat, went up the ladder, and looked around for a crewman to get permission to cross their boat, to get to the bumboat. There was nobody in sight so I just went across the deck to the ladder going down to the bumboat. I found the doorway, which accessed a short stairway down into the bumboat. I didn't see anyone on the deck of the Canadian boat because they were all down in the bumboat!

The bumboat was owned by a fella named Dewey, and he had a roulette wheel installed on his counter. All the Canadians—I think there were six—were playing roulette. Whoever won a certain spin had to buy the others a draft beer. I noticed they were speaking mostly French as they were hooting and hollering when someone had to buy beers.

As I was trying to slip by, one of them shoved a beer in my hand and said, "Here, Jules is buying!"

Well, I'm not one to refuse a beer so I thanked him and moved down the aisle to check out the merchandise. A description of things carried on bumboats is elsewhere in this book, so I won't go into that. I was mostly exploring because I had already gotten what I needed in town. Later, as I was slipping by on my way off the boat, another cheer went up from the Canadians, and someone handed me another beer. At this *point, I was thinking I was going to enjoy my visits aboard bumboats!*

PILOT BOATS

Even the Great Lakes pilot services are different from those on the deep-sea ports. Each port on the Great Lakes does not have its own pilots, which is common with the coastal pilots.

Great Lakes pilot Captain Aaron Menough joined the Navy at the age of seventeen and attended GLMA. He sailed a couple of years deep sea on cruise ships, three years in the Gulf of Mexico on a drill ship, and twelve years on Great Lakes freighters, where he became a captain. He then became a Great Lakes pilot. He explained to me how the pilot business works:

Great Lakes piloting has three districts. D1 is the seaway and through Lake Ontario, D2 covers Port Colborne, all U.S. ports of Lake Erie, and Port Huron. Then D3 covers everything from Port Huron to Chicago, Duluth, and so on—again, only U.S. ports. We share the work with Canadians using a number system one to eight. American pilots take all the odd number jobs, and the Canadians take all the evens. We split the #8 half and half. If the ship comes out of the Welland Canal, which is run by Canada, and it is going to a U.S. port, a United States pilot will always get it. The same thing applies to a Canadian port.

A ship is required to provide twelve hours' notice before needing a pilot. If they blow the call and show up too early, they either wait at anchor or turn circles—running racetracks, an actual type of elongated ship maneuver. So, ETAs are critical and are expected to be accurate, within fifteen minutes. It usually takes seventeen hours to get from Port Colborne to Detroit (the pilot change point). Then it takes another six hours from Detroit to Port Huron. These are simply called "through jobs," because the ship isn't stopping anywhere, just transiting through the river system. If a job is a through-job, that's when

131

it gets assigned a number. So often the dispatcher (whom all fourteen pilots call every morning) might say something like, "We have a #5 coming at 3:00 a.m." Each district has a twenty-four-hour manned dispatch for the twelve-hour call.

Oddly, the three pilot districts don't work as one. Each pilot group is its own association. The pilots are the shareholders, so you buy into the business once registered. If, for example, I take a ship up to Port Huron, and they don't have or can't provide a pilot, that's their problem. I put the ship to anchor at the bottom of Lake Huron and go home. Each pilot pays their expenses—hotels, rental cars, and so on,—like any normal business expenses. The fees charged to the shipping companies for pilotage are all regulated by the U.S. Coast Guard, and there is a lot of oversight and audits. It's all highly regulated and monitored.

The challenges with federal (Federal Marine, foreign flag vessels) is that you are piloting foreign ships, with foreign officers, with sometimes heavy accents. The deep-sea Captains are terrified of blowing the call for the next pilot, and most pilots try to be reassuring, to make sure the call is on time and accurate. In the end, the pilot wants to get home, too.

Often, the foreign crews misunderstand you. I had just finished eating a meal one time, and I told the captain I was full. The mate on watch just heard the word "full," and immediately rang the engine up to full ahead! Another pilot was talking about a hockey game and said, "Oh ya, they won two to three." The wheelsman heard it and just yelled, "Turning to course 223!" So you have to be careful about that.

Also, Lakers use "left" and "right" rudders. If you say that on a salty, they get completely confused. It's the same with knots and miles per hour: mph is only used on Lakers. So the old-school federal pilots say to the new guys, "We have to de-Laker you first." And you don't take any risks on a salty. On a Laker, I was expected to make docks in twenty knots of *wind and commonly did it in thirty knots with no tug assist. We called that maneuver "the hand of the clock" to get into the break wall in high winds. This involved using the thruster to try to hold the bow against the wind and simultaneously putting the rudder hard over and giving the engine "shots" ahead to press yourself up laterally into the wind so that you don't get set down on the break wall. It's a lot of work.*

A STORY FROM BOB OJALA

The Cliffs Victory, *a World War II Victory ship that was converted to a Great Lakes freighter, sailed the Great Lakes for nearly thirty years. I was an ABS class surveyor at the time this occurred (1985), and I was assigned to the following project.*

In 1985, the Cliffs Victory *(aka the* Victory*) was sold to a company in mainland China, purportedly to be used again as a cargo ship. A Chinese American captain named Tommy came to Chicago to oversee the conversion, along with a chief engineer from China. The crewmen were mostly from the Philippines. The ship was ABS classed, so all of the class and regulatory surveys had to be brought up to date—other than dry-docking, which was going to be required in about six months. They planned to reach China and dry-dock the vessel there.*

I made two visits each week to the Victory *for nearly three months over the fall, and the shipowner wanted to leave before they closed the St. Lawrence Seaway in December. The weather was getting bad and all were worried they would not be done in time to beat the closure.*

The crew was not used to cold weather and was not being paid enough to buy warm clothes. My wife collected old coats in our neighborhood to give to the crew members. Because they were not familiar with snow and ice, the crew did not clean the ice from the deck, and they did not use salt. One day I was on deck and coming down a stairway when my feet lost traction, and I bounced down about five steps on my butt, breaking my tailbone. This required a trip to a chiropractor to get it straightened out. Not fun!

I would frequently eat aboard the ship, and Captain Tommy refused to let me use a fork. He said anyone eating in his dining room, needed to learn how to use chopsticks or eat with their fingers! It took a while, but I did get quite proficient with chopsticks. I use chopsticks to this day when eating Asian food. The crew served grilled squid during many of those meals, in a soy sauce marinade. Much better than deep-fried calamari! One weekend, Captain Tommy invited me to dinner, and he asked me to bring my wife along. Carol was always adventurous and enjoyed Captain Tommy. She spoke about him for years.

The ship was operating on a very tight budget. The new Chinese owners were cutting corners in every possible way. When I asked Captain Tommy for the new ship's name to be used on the certificates being prepared, he said it was SAVIC . I did not question the name but wondered why they chose such a strange name. When leaving the ship that day, the crew was painting on the bow and I then understood the new name: ~~CLIFF~~SAVIC~~TORY~~.

The owners even saved money when repainting a new name! They just painted over the CLIFF and the TORY with black paint and added one new white letter, the A, to form the new name.

When the ship was finally finished, they ordered two Great Lakes pilots to take them out of the Lakes, because Captain Tommy did not have a Great Lakes pilotage endorsement on his license. When the pilots arrived, I gave the captain his class, load line, and SOLAS certificates. I could see that one of the pilots was not impressed by the competency of the crew, and he used this as his excuse to leave and make it home before Christmas.

The next morning in the ABS Chicago office, we received a call from the new pilot, saying something was wrong with the ship. They had told the chief engineer to ballast the ship down, and the ship began to vibrate badly. The pilots had reached Milwaukee and were lying at anchor. I was instructed to go to Milwaukee to see what was going on!

Arriving in Milwaukee around noon, after a two-hour drive, the ship's agent had arranged a tugboat to get out to the ship. I had to board the ship using the pilot's ladder, which is a vertical rope ladder with wood rungs hanging down the side of the ship. Since I had never used a pilot's ladder before, the tug captain gave instructions to grab the side ropes as high as possible, timing it with the waves to be high up the ladder. He also instructed me to pull the ladder tight into my chest. That is not me at the end of the chapter, but after my first experience on a pilot's ladder, I respect the pilots who have to do this in all kinds of weather.

The waves were not bad that day, but the lake steam was rising off the water, giving the ship an eerie look, like it was emerging out of the fog. I timed my grab correctly, but my feet slipped off the rungs. The lake fog was freezing on the rungs, making them slippery. I hung there by my two hands for what seemed like an eternity until I was able to find some traction with my feet. Luckily, my weight was reasonable in those days, and I was also in good physical shape. Again, the crew's inexperience with cold weather caused these problems. I was lucky not to have fallen into the lake, or even worse, as the tug was surging beneath me, it could have crushed my legs.

This pilot's ladder experience was useful numerous times over the rest of my career. I always dreaded having to use them, but sometimes there was no other alternative. Wearing a bulky life jacket makes it difficult to climb a pilot's ladder. The tug captain's last instruction in Milwaukee—about holding the ladder tight to my chest—is important. Because the pilot's ladder has no solid side rail, only rope, if you let your arms extend forward, the rope ladder pulls away from the ship's side and you cannot climb (note that in the photo at the end of this chapter). I now use an inflatable life jacket, which is thin when not inflated. It makes this procedure much easier. Safely aboard the ship that day in Milwaukee, I told the crew to thaw out the ladder before my departure.

While approaching the ship by tug, the cause of the vibration problem was evident. The bow of the ship was deep in the water and the stern was up, exposing a good portion of the propeller. This caused of the vibration. Although ABS was not responsible for instructing the crew on operations, showing the chief engineer the crossover valve, used to flood the aft ballast tanks, which he had not opened, was the simple solution. The ship then evened out, ready to sail.

The ship had planned to stop in Detroit for a load of scrap steel, the income from which would have paid for the trip to China. One of the pilots had left the ship after the vibration experience and the remaining pilot had requested another man to replace him. He explained to the captain that stopping in Detroit could potentially trap the ship in the Great Lakes until the seaway opened the following spring. We believe that they left without stopping in Detroit, but never heard the end of the story.

The sad thing about this story is that the ship was cut up for scrap after reaching China and never made another voyage.

Typically, when a pilot is needed for departure from another port, such as Duluth-Superior Harbor, for example, the pilot's association will send a pilot there to board the vessel. However, in some busier ports, such as Duluth, a pilot may have taken a ship to Duluth and must remain there for the next departure.

The pilot is charged with protecting the public interest. The pilot boards a vessel via a rope ladder hanging on the side of the ship while the ship is moving. When on the bridge, he directs the navigation of the vessel in conjunction with the master of the vessel. This means that through his skill, experience, and training, the pilot is responsible for safely maneuvering a ship to and from the berth without incident. In coastwise ports, the pilot boards the vessel when it arrives at the sea buoy just outside the port. On the Great Lakes, a pilot is aboard every ocean vessel during its entire transit on the Lakes. In addition to navigation and ship-handling duties, the modern-day pilot also makes sure that pollutants are not dumped into our waters as well as monitoring the vessel for potential homeland security issues. The pilot is usually the only U.S. or Canadian citizen aboard the vessel.

Pilots go through extensive training before becoming members of the Great Lakes Pilots Association. In addition to the U.S. Coast Guard requirements for federal pilot registration, a potential candidate must go through a three-year training program before he is fully qualified to pilot vessels in our entire district.

Great Lakes pilots are among the best ship handlers in the world, and our safety record is testament to that fact.

RESEARCH BOAT

Captain Stormi Sutter is another of our female Great Lakes captains, originally from and still living in Michigan. Stormi works in a very unusual part of the Great Lakes maritime world. She is the captain of the Research Vessel *Stanford H. Smith,* working with the U.S. Fish and Wildlife Service in Kewaunee, Wisconsin.

After ten years in the Navy, Stormi was injured and began looking for another career. She eventually enrolled in the Great Lakes Maritime Academy and graduated in 2007.

Stormi occasionally fills in as a tugboat captain when not working her normal job, and she is well respected by the other Great Lakes captains who know her. She also takes relief jobs off the Great Lakes during the winter, works on new vessel delivery crews, and worked with the Army Corps of Engineers for a while. When not working, Stormi is part owner, of a disc jockey business back home.

Stormi's time with the Army Corps of Engineers was spent working on dredges in both the New Orleans and Portland districts. She changed jobs for a lot of reasons, but because I have also worked for the Army Corps, I loved her statement that it was "run by people who had dirt on one another for thirty-plus years." I experienced the same mindset during my eight and a half years with the Army Corps, and yes, it is impossible to change that mindset.

1. Westcott Mail Boat in Detroit, Michigan.

2. Mail Boat leaving the freighter after making delivery.

News Trib excerpt Aug 3,1939 (copy pg 2 pic Service Boat to be launched today) 55ft launch, built at the National Steel co yards in Duluth, for use in servicing ships with supplies . . named Marine Trader, the launch will be used by Kaner Bros of Superior who operate another similar boat (note-bumboat).

3. Marine Trader, bumboat at Duluth, Minnesota.

4. Kaner Brothers bumboat at Duluth, Minnesota.

5. Bumboat at ore docks, so crew could do some shopping.

6. Typical Great Lakes Pilot Boat.

8. Captain Stormi Sutter, Great Lakes and deep-sea Master.

7. Boarding the ship, using a Pilot's Ladder.

9. Research Vessel, captained by Stormi Sutter.

CHAPTER 8

Sailing and Its Effects On the Family

All through the previous chapters, the problems of the sailor were emphasized. Yes, it was and is a tough life for the sailors, but the sailors' wives and children also suffered, almost like a one-parent family.

Sailors today are still away from home for sixty days at a time, but that hardly compares to the nine- to eleven-month contracts that existed before the mid-1970s. I remember looking forward to a letter from my father when I was a young child. Occasionally, we got a phone call. My mother did the talking, but my sister and I were next to the phone, waiting to say hello.

In my own life working aboard ships, I saw pay phones on the ore docks with the line of men waiting for their turn to call home. In fact, the crews on the large ocean cruise ships still wait in line to call their families in the Philippines or Romania, because they don't have unlimited calling cell phones like American sailors have.

The following story from Captain Ed Wiltse brings back memories.

Another thing I remember from the old days is not having any communications home from the boat. When we would get into port, the guys off watch would pile off the ladder and head up to the pay phone, usually at the end of the dock, to call home. Often, the dock was a dirty or muddy mess. The phone booth was usually located under a structure or conveyor belt, and it was always filthy as well. But we didn't know any better.

Nowadays, the younger guys demand constant contact with the outside world, including internet access for shopping via Amazon, or whatever website. They can do their banking, and whatever, twenty-four hours a day, no matter where the ship happens to be.

When I started sailing, you were lucky if you were able to talk with a loved one once a week or so. Otherwise, there was no contact ashore, except for an occasional letter via the mail boat in Detroit, or the Soo post office.

I remember one trip when I was the third mate on the steamer the *Edward L. Ryerson*. It was late fall in 1989, and we were loading taconite up at the DMIR dock in Duluth, Minnesota. The *Ryerson* could load 26,000 tons of taconite in three hours or less if the dock was charged with enough cargo and fully ready for us. So if you happened to be on watch when the ship tied up, you possibly wouldn't get an opportunity to run up to the phone to call home unless you could get someone to stand by for you.

By the time I got off watch, we had less than an hour or so to finish the load. So as quickly as I could, I climbed down the ladder and walked under the chutes on the ore dock and headed for the phone booth. It was by the inner end of the dock. As I got closer, I could see the light at the top of the phone booth through the murky dark shadows under the ore dock. In front of the phone booth, I could see one of the guys talking on the phone and the backs of four other crew members who were waiting in line for their turn at the phone.

As I waited, a few other guys showed up to wait their turn at the phone, as well. Once in a while, one of the guys in line would grumble a little at the guy on the phone if he was taking too long. By the time I got my chance, I quickly dialed my home number, and the phone calling card number, hoping to hear my wife's voice on the other end of the line, just so I could tell her I was OK, and to find out how things were at home. Maddeningly, the phone line buzzed an intermittent busy signal.

Damn, I thought, hanging up the receiver and stepping out of the phone booth to return to the back of the line.

Looking at my watch, I realized we had less than twenty minutes left until sailing time, according to the sailing board on the ship. There were two guys ahead of me. Would I get another shot to talk to my wife before I had to return to the ship?

By the time I had another chance on the phone, I had less than five minutes left. I dialed again and the phone rang and rang. There was no answer. I remember hustling back to the ship, wondering if everything was okay at home, and hoping I would get a chance to speak with her when we got down to Indiana Harbor.

That was the way communications worked back then. Unless you got an emergency call via WLC on the VHF radio out of Rogers City. WLC would patch a landline phone call through to a ship out on the lake via the VHF radio. Of course, when WLC called a ship and asked them to switch to a working channel, every mate on watch on every other ship in the vicinity—if they didn't have much going on—would also switch over and listen in to your phone call.

On some quiet evenings or late nights, it was quite entertaining to listen to some woman chew out her husband or boyfriend for something or another. Sometimes the news from ashore was tragic, like the death of a parent or some other family member. It was kind of like listening in on an old party line phone.

The officers were able to arrange for their wives to sail with them for limited amounts of time. Some wives hated to sail, *and if they had young children, it was tough to leave them home during these trips.*

There is a photo at the end of the chapter, showing my parents, Matt and Ann Ojala, sitting on a hatch cover during a summer ride for my mother. She hated riding ship because she was always seasick. I must have inherited that tendency from her.

MARRIAGE FAILURES

Divorce is an affliction of most sailors, both Great Lakes and deep sea. Some of them manage to remain married while sailing, but then divorce when they retire. The reason, in my opinion, is largely due to the fact that their wives ran their household for years while the husband sailed. She had other interests in her life, such as clubs, hobbies, school events for the children, and, like my mother, singing in a women's club choir at various events. However, when the sailor was home between contracts, or eventually when he retired, the wife was expected to give up all her interests and devote most, if not all, of her time to her sailor husband! It is easy to see the arguments and dissatisfaction that resulted between the sailor and his wife.

My parents divorced after fifteen years of marriage, and my father once told me he only knew one man whom he had sailed with who was still married to his first wife. I have known numerous sailors throughout the years, both Great Lakes and deep sea, and most were divorced.

The following comments are from Captain Ed Wiltse, who sailed for several years with the deck crew, eventually becoming a captain. Ed did not want to continue, knowing it would eventually affect his marriage:

> *Yes, the life of a sailor can be difficult on a marriage. I learned the same thing about high divorce rates among those who sailed for many years.*

Some of those who stayed married had what I thought were strange relationships, where it seemed to be more of a financial arrangement than a marriage.

I remember a long-time captain I knew and respected when I was just starting. He sailed for well over thirty years and often spoke enthusiastically of his planned retirement as he got down to his last few seasons. When he finally retired and went home to spend his remaining years with his wife, he quickly found that she had developed a full life over the years, and his presence was sometimes not convenient or appreciated. Shortly after he left the boats, he took a part-time job as a delivery truck driver for something to do to get out of the house.

It seemed the golden years with her that he had looked forward to for many years while on the boats was not to be. His story made an impression on me, and I have tried to learn from his example and not end up the same way.

I polled the contributors to this book (all of the sailors), and from their perspectives, their children and those of their friends have turned out well, despite their fathers' long absences. There certainly may be exceptions to this, but no worse than in any other profession.

In some instances, particularly on car ferries, the children—or the entire family—get to make trips aboard ship, and their father can spend some quality time with them when he is off watch, or during time in port. This opportunity is rare on the freighters due to safety regulations, but some shipping companies allowed children to sail at age fourteen but most are age eighteen, which was the case for my father's company.

In my opinion, my father's absence made me more independent and self-sufficient. My mother guided me but did not "over-mother" me. I learned to think for myself because my father was seldom there to ask for advice.

FAMILIES' PERSPECTIVE

During the research for this book, I tried to read as many books written by Great Lakes sailors as were available and found two additional books written by sailors' family members. Although these books did not change my overall opinions greatly, they did show another side of the family experience, which were different from most, (including mine). The reason for the difference is because some shipping fleets, such as Hanna Mining, tended to make weekly trips between Duluth-Superior Harbor in Lake Superior and the lower Lakes, carrying iron ore to the steel mills. Because of these regular trips, the sailors' families who happened to live in the Duluth/Superior area were able to see their husbands and fathers regularly, although those visits were short.

A good book on this subject is *Widow of the Waves* by Bev Jamison, published by Savage Press. She describes her thirty-three years of marriage during her husband's thirty-six-year sailing career, and their happy life together, which continued into retirement. She does comment on the fact that other crew members, who did not live near one of their regularly visited ports, did not have the same opportunity.

Bev also described some of her twenty-five to thirty trips aboard her husband's ships, including some with their children, which was not allowed by most companies.

Another great book is *Ship Captain's Daughter* by Ann M. Lewis, published by the Wisconsin Historical Society Press. Ann's father was a captain, and she rode her father's ships, along with her mother, on many occasions. Ann took one last trip on her father's ore carrier after graduating from college, and the following paragraph is a great description of how tough life can be as a sailor, particularly in the busy waterways of the Great Lakes. As a young girl, Ann thought her father's life was exciting. As an adult, she sees the toll it takes on a sailor.

The following text from Ann Lewis's book is reprinted with the publisher's permission.

148

I looked at him. He was still tall, thin, and handsome, but wrinkles were beginning to form around his eyes and mouth. In his short-sleeved shirt, I could see that his tattoo was fading. The yellow in the snake's eyes had almost disappeared. I thought back to the night when Dad had become a captain, how excited he was. I wondered if he still felt that way. How many hundreds of nights had he stayed up? How many rivers had he navigated in fog? How many tense landings had he made? How many wild storms had he sailed through? How many family events had he missed? How many fleet managers had he dealt with? The older I got, the harder his life seemed. I wondered if the older man would choose the young man's dream again.

Both books show the best scenarios for a sailor's family. However, most sailors and their families could only wish to have such good times with their father or husband. Only a small number of such lucky family members existed prior to the recent union contracts.

1. Author's Mom & Dad, when she was riding ship.

CHAPTER 9

Great Lakes Car Ferries–How Are They Different From Ore Carriers?

Mike Braybrook, my collaborator on this book, was in the Navy for four years. He spent some of that aboard ships in Vietnam, the Mediterranean, the Caribbean, and the Atlantic. Plus, he sailed the Great Lakes on both ore carriers and on car ferries, for a total of thirty-six years as a merchant mariner.

Mike sailed on the original Train Car Carriers—also known as car ferries—which carried mostly train cars but also some passenger cars and passengers. He also sailed on the passenger car ferries after the train car business ended, carrying passengers and their autos, plus some semi-trucks.

Besides the physical differences and the bulk cargoes versus the railcars, automobiles, and passengers, life for the crews on the car ferries was also quite different. Many of the ferries sailed across Lake Michigan between several specific repetitive ports, so the crew occasionally got to make a quick run home while the ferry was unloading and reloading. These visits were short but at least they got to see their family.

Another picture at the end of this chapter, which is part of my collection of Great Lakes Ship postcards, shows the car ferry *City of*

Milwaukee on Lake Michigan. It was reproduced for Grand Trunk from a painting by Russ Porter.

There was also a pay difference, with car ferry sailors earning as much as 30 percent less than the ore boat sailors. This was driven by the unions, who seemed to look after the interests of the ore boat crews more than the car ferry crews.

Car ferries did tend to sail year-round, but the crews worked twenty days on and eight days off, which was the railroad work schedule. The car ferry crews also started with a one-week vacation each season, which increased with longevity, up to three weeks per year.

WEATHER AND CAR FERRIES

Car ferries were built for tough duty operations. You will see in the following story from Mike Braybrook that winter operations were tough.

Well into the winter, when the Lakers and most tugs were in lay-up, the car ferries continued their runs across Lake Michigan. The car ferries were designed with an ice-class hull and propellers, so they could operate year-round.

The roughest job in the winter had to be the car handlers. Because of the frequent rough water, the railcars required full gear to keep them stable during the trip across the lakes [see the photos referenced in the next section]. There were two lengths of screw jacks they had to manhandle: an eighty-pounder and a hundred-pounder. Heavy chains also had to be wrapped around the tank cars. When the railcars were pushed aboard, they were often covered with snow and ice, which would start falling to the deck where the car handlers were working. This made for a miserable time of it, as they sometimes had to crawl through it, and then the ice-cold water would run off the cars down their necks.

Winter sailing would even have an effect down in the boiler and engine rooms, as well. When the temperature would fall to the teens or lower outside, the ventilation fans would be cut down to a minimum.

There still had to be some ventilation or there would be condensation problems. There was a vent duct that came down between the steam engines, just above the throttles. Even though the fan was shut off, cold outside air slowly dropped down through the ductwork, causing icicles to form at the bottom. This was a very odd thing to see in an engine room.

Out in the boiler room, you would think it would be hot all the time, but not in the winter when it was below zero out on the lake. While the fireman and coal passer were cleaning fires, they would have to turn on the vent fans to clear out the smoke and dust caused by that operation, and then would shut them off afterward. It was not uncommon to see them put on a jacket and drag a stool over by a boiler drum to warm up.

One severe winter, the *City of Midland* was battling heavy ice just outside the break walls at Ludington. The chief and the engineer on watch were getting constant orders on their respective telegraphs, as the captain tried to work his way through the ice. Suddenly, we could feel a rumble from back aft, and then the starboard engine took off running wild, till the engineer shut down the throttle. I almost had to laugh at the look of bewilderment on his face.

For a couple of seconds, that big steam engine sounded like a sewing machine! Later we found out one of the propeller blades had broken off in the ice and had lodged in the hull. The other blades broke off as they came around and hit it.

Once a car ferry loses the use of an engine while in the ice, they can no longer maneuver, so we were stuck there till the ice-breaking Coast Guard Cutter, tug *Raritan* came to help us into the harbor.

Three great photos at the end of this chapter were supplied by Ken Ottmann, showing how the car ferries had to battle ice on Lake Michigan."

JOBS ON CAR FERRIES

The majority of jobs on the Lakers and car ferries are much the same. They both carried captains, mates, ABs, deckhands, chief engineers, assistant engineers, oilers, and wipers, as well as galley crew. The car ferries, however, specifically the coal-burning ones, had a few extra types of jobs. In the engine department, the extra jobs consisted of watertenders, firemen, coal passers, and junior engineers.

Watertenders sailed because car ferries were passenger-carrying vessels, with the boilers located in a separate compartment from the main engines, and the auxiliaries. Those compartments also included the boiler feed water pumps, which the watertenders also operated and maintained. At their station in the engine room, they had remote boiler water level indicators, which they would monitor to maintain the proper water level in each boiler.

Firemen sailed to tend the fires in the boiler furnaces, pull ashes out of the ash pits after the fires had been dumped, operate and maintain the mechanical stokers, and monitor the steam pressure.

Coal passers sailed because the conveyor room, which was under the ship's coal bunkers, was separate from the boiler room. Their job was to move stoker coal from the main bunkers to the day bunkers over the boilers, first thing every watch. They did this by using a system of three types of conveyors. Then during the watch, they assisted the firemen in cleaning fires and pulling ash from the ash pits.

Another rated position that sailed on the ferries was the junior engineer. Most cargo ships on the Lakes carried an extra assistant engineer who was a day man, responsible for repair and maintenance. The car ferries carried two junior engineers because of all the extra equipment aboard.

In the deck department, two extra jobs were needed—car handlers and a patrolman.

The car handlers were responsible for stabilizing the railcars on the car deck using jacks, chains, and wheel clamps, so they wouldn't shift around during rough weather. In the summer, whenever the lake was calm, the strings of railcars only required wheel clamps on the end of each string, so the car handlers were used for painting and general cleaning maintenance.

Being passenger-carrying vessels, ferries were required by Coast Guard regulations to carry a patrolman who made rounds through the boat at night, mainly for fire and flooding security.

In the steward's department, extra jobs were required to take care of the passengers, including stewardess, cabin maid, pantryman, plankman, and dining room waiter.

The plankman is an unusual position, probably only seen on Great Lakes passenger ferries. When the boat pulled into the slip, it was the plankman's job to pull the gangway—or gangplank—over from the dock to the main deck and secure it. He then stood watch and assisted the passengers aboard and helped with luggage when needed. At some point, the steward would take over for the plankman, because the plankman's job also included the responsibility of bringing bags of clean linen aboard and taking soiled linen off.

The boats also carried a purser and an assistant purser who sold tickets to any passengers who hadn't already bought them in the ticket office ashore. They also rented out staterooms and were responsible for all money held aboard the boat.

TYPICAL OILER'S DAY

Mike Braybrook describes a typical day in an oiler's life aboard ship:

An oiler's day on a car ferry started with coffee, although that's pretty universal for any watchstander on any ship. Being coal burners, the Ludington-based boats had watertenders standing watch in the engine room, and they were tasked with making fresh coffee for the oncoming watch.

As an oiler, I would troop down to the engine room with the rest of the reliefs and draw a cup of coffee from the big electric pot. It was rare, but some guys who didn't drink coffee would have a soda instead. That usually had caffeine so the effect was the same.

I would slowly get my wits about me as I drank the coffee and listened to the oiler I was relieving as he told me what was going on with the plant. He would relay info about water levels in the different tanks, and maybe a bearing somewhere that seemed to be a bit warmer than usual. He would share any orders the chief may have left, and if we were nearing port, he would say about what time to expect the twenty-minute call, which was a toot on the small steam work whistle in the upper engine room.

That whistle let us know we were twenty minutes from the break wall and gave us time to ring the chief engineer on the sound-powered phone. The chief needed ample time to wake up and make his way down before we came into port.

Also, we needed time to switch over a few things. But anyway, after getting all the needed info from the other oiler, he was relieved and I would take over the watch. There was no need to dive into it right away, as one might need to have a second cup of coffee and engage in a bit of small talk with the other guys on the watch.

Regardless of whether you were underway or tied up in a slip, the first thing the oiler did was make a round through the engine room. That was done to check every piece of machinery that is operating, check water levels in tanks and double bottoms, and also make note of all temperatures and pressures. These would all need to be put in the engine room log later. The ship's service steam turbine generator had a log that must be kept up.

Later in the watch, the oiler needed time to leave the engine room to also make a round. It was the oiler's job to go back aft, through the shaft alleys, check the shaft spring bearings, and continue back to the steering gear flat. There, he would *check the hydraulic pumps, electric motors, rudder stock packing gland seal, and the propeller shaft seals, which had to be greased with a pneumatic greaser.*

Then it was on to the stack above to check the induced draft fans and the steam turbines that turn them. Directly behind that was the main ventilation room where there were several electric motors and fan bearings to be checked.

On the way back to the engine room, it was necessary to stop by the galley to see what goodies the galley crew was putting out. There were always things available to eat between meals, and the coffee was always on. Also, it was a good place to pick up the latest gossip and hear the latest news before it makes its way around the boat.

There is a picture from my postcard collection at the end of this chapter, showing the Carferry *Ann Arbor No. 5* departing Manitowoc, Wisconsin.

1. Three old ferries at Ludington, Michigan.

2. Carferry City of Milwaukee post card.

3. Fireman 'pulling fires' on coal-fired carferry.

4. Two carferries working in the ice off Michigan.

5. Three carferries working in the ice off Michigan.

6. Crew member watching ice operation.

7. Rail car jacks and chocks on rail car ferry.

8. Carferry Ann Arbor IV leaving Manitowoc, Wisconsin.

CHAPTER 10

Unusual Events

During our first meeting, Mike Braybrook told me a story related to a photograph I had seen in his ship files on his computer.

Every merchant ship has an emergency generator (see the photo at the end of this chapter), usually installed high on the ship, sometimes in a small compartment inside the exhaust stack. The generator is designed to supply power to the bare essentials on a ship, to allow communications, emergency lighting, and very basic ship operations, under emergency conditions.

The generator is tested frequently, usually weekly, but cannot be tested under actual loaded conditions on a car ferry while passengers are aboard. The Coast Guard usually requires a load test once a year, or sometimes at a quarterly inspection, but those load tests are generally quite short.

During Mike's time as a junior engineer aboard a passenger ferry, they began to lose steam pressure to their water feed pumps, generators, and other equipment, due to plugged steam lines. The main engines then lost power as well, so the ship was dead in the water. This is where Mike's story begins:

As designed, the emergency generator started automatically, and the emergency lights came on. Luckily, it was a calm evening, and the ferry was not too far out of port, so the captain called a tug service to come out for an assist tow back into port. It was a weekend, so the towing company said it might take them a while to gather a crew, but with good weather and the emergency lights there was no danger.

Then things started going wrong. The chief engineer had a junior engineer go up and check the operation of the emergency generator periodically. During one check, the junior engineer noticed some unusual noise coming out of the generator, so he called down to the chief on the sound-powered phone to have him come up and listen to it.

Not long after the chief got there, it started to clatter. Smoke and sparks started to come out of the air vents. The epoxy binder around the windings had started coming loose, and when the guys thought it was going to fly apart, one jumped out the starboard door of the generator room. The other jumped out the port side door, cussing loudly as he went! The chief had hit the emergency shutoff on the diesel engine, so when it came to a stop, there was dead silence.

At that point, the captain, who was standing in the open doorway of the pilothouse only about fifteen feet away, suggested they stop swearing because the passengers at either end of the boat could hear them!

The irony of this was, when the emergency generator was needed the most, right at dusk, was when it decided to fail.

Now with the entire plant shut down, none of the pumps were working, including the sanitary pump that supplied water pressure to the toilets. The cruise director came up to me and said the passengers were using the toilets, thinking that they would still flush. I went below and got a couple of five-gallon buckets and some heaving line, and told him to have his boys drop them over the side of the boat into the lake and bring up water to be dumped into the toilets, which would then flush them down to the holding tanks.

At this point, some excitable lady saw them with the water buckets over the side and got a bit shook up. She used her cell phone to call the Two Rivers Coast Guard station, which was in sight of the boat, and said the boat must be leaking, as they were bucketing water over the side! The Coast Guard, of course, had been staying in contact with the captain and called him to ask what was going on. After he explained the buckets, they all laughed.

As it got darker, the cruise director had the gift shop attendants retrieve souvenir candles from their storeroom and put them on the tables in the main passenger lounge for lighting. One crew member quipped, "We should charge the passengers extra because they are now on a candlelight cruise."

Later, in hindsight, that was considered a bad idea, as there was no firefighting capability with the fire pumps down.

Long after dark, we finally spotted the tug coming down from Sturgeon Bay to tow us back into Manitowoc so that we could disembark the passengers and vehicles. Then someone recognized the next problem: getting the sea gate open to allow the vehicles off, as there was no power to operate the winch. The chief came up with the ingenious idea of jerry-rigging a hand-operated crank off the end of the shaft, on the electric motor powering the winch. The winch was geared way down, so ten full turns on the hand crank only brought the sea gate up about one-quarter of an inch. There was a tour bus on the boat, so it took about three hours of cranking to get the sea gate high enough to let it off.

The sea gate winch room was just forward of the aft pilothouse and many of the crew took turns on the crank, so it was turning constantly. With the door open, passengers could look in and see what was going on. It was almost like a Huckleberry Finn moment, because some passengers thought it would be fun to give it a try, and the crew was happy to oblige!

It was around 2:00 a.m. when the tug finally maneuvered the boat into the slip, and the passengers and vehicles were taken off. Then at daybreak, the tug pulled us back out of the slip and started for Ludington, where repairs would be completed.

Another great car ferry "happening" occurred during the one-hundredth anniversary of Harley-Davidson in 2003. People from everywhere came to Milwaukee. Many of them wanted to avoid the drive through Chicago. That desire for many guys to be on a ship, also drew those Harley riders to the ride the carferry *Badger*.

Two of the photos at the end of this chapter show the entire car deck of the Badger filled with motorcycles—we assume all Harleys. The other photo shows the riders coming aboard at Ludington. The exact number of cycles is not known, but there were well over four hundred on board.

"The *Badger* can carry a maximum of 620 people including the crew, so this is one of the rare times that they maxed out with passengers rather than vehicles," Mike Braybrook told me.

That trip was one of the quickest unloads. All the bikers went down to the car deck, untied their bikes, and were mostly ready to go when the mate gave the go-ahead to start leaving the car deck. There was a steady stream of them riding off.

"The only other time the boat unloaded that fast was when the National Guard chartered the boat for a trip, so there was nothing but Army vehicles aboard. When it was time to unload, all the vehicles were manned and running, and there were military police (MPs) posted at several places to direct them, so the unloading was fast," Mike said.

He continued, "The only downside was the car deck was choked with diesel smoke, which took a while to clear before the crew could start driving the next load of cars aboard."

Not all motorcycle experiences were good on the car ferries, however. This next story from Mike not only shows the occasional trouble that can occur with passengers, but also how a good captain can deal with it.

This story, which took place in the late 1950s, involved a Hells Angels–type wannabe motorcycle gang going across the lake on the City of Midland during a night trip. They were walking around the decks after a few drinks playing badass and throwing chairs, trash cans, and fire axes over the side, causing general chaos. When word of this got to the captain, he went down to the fo'c'sle, gathered the deck crew who were off watch, and told them to go down to the car deck.

They lined up all the motorcycles along the stern and raised the sea gate about ten feet. The captain then proceeded to the cross-ship passageway and locked the door to the stairs leading down to the car deck. At this point, he was ready to go look for the bikers.

Once he found them, he asked who the "road captain" was. Once he identified himself, the captain led him aft to the stern, overlooking the car deck below. The captain pointed down to his crew standing among the bikes, each with a jack bar in hand, and told the road captain that if his gang caused any more trouble during the trip, the ship's crew was going to start pushing the bikes off the stern into the lake one by one. The road captain's bike would be the first to go. Needless to say, there was no more trouble from the bikers.

A smart captain is great to have under all adverse conditions!

Here are a few more unusual stories from Captain Aaron Menough. You will think you only have animal problems in your home? Well, think again! The first story is quite eerie, being in a pilothouse alone and thinking the ship may be haunted, or worse:

In 2004, I was second mate on the McKee Sons. The McKee Sons was an Integrated Tug-Barge, or ITB. It was a really efficient boat that could haul up to six different cargoes at once. It also unloaded quickly, making it valuable in the eyes of the office.

I remember having a long week of short sand runs between Grand Haven and St. Joseph, Michigan. The turnaround time is short with just a few hours between docks. There was only enough time to catch a short nap at best. In addition to the light backhauls, we would have to climb down into the steep cargo holds and kick out thousands of tons of sand with our feet, hands, and whatever else we could use. After doing this once, which usually took about five to six hours, you were worn out. Do this three or four times in a week and you were burned out.

We fought our way through all the loads successfully and were all looking forward to some downtime, traveling from the Chicago area back up Lake Michigan, which is roughly a twenty-four-hour haul.

I arrived for my night watch, which was from 11:45 p.m. until 3:45 a.m. I was looking forward to the calm summer night. I made the passage through Gray's Reef without any problems, and then made a right turn towards the Mackinac Bridge. Even two hours away, the mighty Mac's bridge lights burned bright along the cables of the five-mile-long suspension bridge.

I sat poised in my chair and turned the helm into manual, so I would be steering by hand, instead of autopilot, while going under the bridge. With no traffic in sight, this was when sailing was at its most enjoyable.

I prepared the logbook for the Mackinac Bridge entry by checking the weather. I walked about the pilothouse, studied the barometer, and recorded all the readings. I spun the wind wheel around and recorded the direction and velocity. After viewing my magnetic heading, I sat down again, perched in my little chair, making sure everything was normal.

In the pitch-black space of that pilothouse, something suddenly made a pass at my face. At first, I thought there was another person in the pilothouse messing with me. I looked around the room, turned the flashlight on, but nothing. Everything was right where I left it.

Another pass about the back of my head! My heart was pumping! My head was turning all about. The bridge was getting closer. I turned around in my chair so much I was disoriented. The entire five-mile-long Mackinac Bridge, merely hundreds of yards in front of me, was closing in on me at fourteen miles per hour. What should I do? I didn't want to flip the ship back into autopilot under the bridge. That's just bad navigating. Something was in the room with me!

"Tim!" I shouted. "Is that you?"

Our engineer was notorious for playing jokes, but it also made no sense that he would randomly come up to the pilothouse at 2:00 a.m. Even this joke was way too elaborate for him.

I tried not to think of any ghost stories I had heard in the past. I also knew too well that the McKee Sons was built in the 1940s and was a troop transport ship. It made a few trips to North Africa under the name Marine Angel, and then the war ended. It sailed stateside again before it was converted into a cargo vessel. It eventually worked its way to the Great Lakes and still runs to this day. Perhaps somebody died all those years ago and was now coming back to let it be known: their house of eternal dwelling should not be infringed upon.

I held my post, however. It took only ten minutes to get around the corner of the bridge buoys so that I could work my way to Poe Reef. I quickly made the turn and put the boat back in autopilot. I grabbed the first flashlight I could find and started walking around the pilothouse. Again! Something just brushed the top of my hair! I went to the other side of the pilothouse and started a search. Nothing to be found. I went to the other side again: nothing. Yet, something was in the air.

The front half of the pilothouse was separated from the back half by a long wall with an office area. I didn't want to go back there. It was creepy and dark. Armed with nothing but a flashlight, I manned up and went for it.

Few things on earth are ever timed so well, and this was one of them. As I stepped and turned into the doorway, the object of terror literally hit me in the face, smacking me in the mouth! Up to that moment, I didn't know what "it" was. I smartly identified the sensation of a rubbery and furry substance against my lips. The sensation quickly wrapped around the sides of my cheeks, and I felt two tiny little pokes around my ears.

I threw my arms up in the air. The flashlight flew, cartwheeling up into the air, then back to the floor again.

"BLAGGGGGHHHHHH!" was the only thing I said, and with extreme disgust!

Now I was upset. I turned on all the lights in the pilothouse. I didn't care anymore where that ship went. I didn't care if I ran over every buoy in the South Passage. I didn't care one bit if I smashed into the lighthouse at Fourteen Foot Shoal. (Well, I did!)

I lit the place up like the Fourth of July and saw the little brown bat pick himself up off the floor. I instantly felt horrible about the collision my furry friend and I just had, but also the horrible taste of his little rubbery wings and furry little torso in my mouth, which I can still recall to this day.

After this traumatic experience, I took a few deep breaths and shut the lights off again, so that the poor bat could recover. I thought it would make him more comfortable to be in the dark, and he would soon be on his way out. I propped open every door we had in the pilothouse so he could stumble his way home. No doubt he would tell his little bat friends a story about an obnoxious sailor and that he did, in fact, get "one of those dirty people" all over his little body due to a sonar flight gone bad.

I did hear a few more noises as he regained his ability to fly again. I also thought if I just held perfectly still that his chances of making it out would be significantly greater. As my watch came to an end, I heard no more passes.

This next story from Captain Aaron is also not what you'd expect to find happening aboard a cargo ship:

Another occupational hazard I recall is a story about loading at Cargill in Cleveland, Ohio. Cargill is a huge underground salt mine, which extends miles underneath Lake Erie. It turns out these are some of the largest salt deposits in the country, and even the world. I've never been down in the mines, but, almost daily, we witness the amount of infrastructure involved in an operation that large.

Working only shipside, I've never seen past the dock. The salt is mined far below, brought up to the surface, then treated and either packaged in bags for resale or taken up to the conveyor belts to be loaded into the ships.

The ship loading rig is right in the middle of the parking lot, and the land it sits on is part of a small island at the front end of Cleveland Harbor. It's also connected to a small marina and public park, with trees and rocks everywhere. It's not uncommon to see little critters all over the place.

On what was a normal day of loading, one of our little friends (a raccoon) somehow managed to make it through the plant, the parking lots, and the bulldozers to the conveyor belts. As my friends sat and stood by the loading hatch watching the salt go in, they witnessed the little raccoon shooting off the end of the loading belt and plunging thirty to forty feet into the cargo hold.

"Hey, mate?" the loader said.

"*Ya go ahead, this is the boat,*" our mate yelled over the radio.

"*Ya, I think a raccoon just went into your cargo hold,*" replied the loader.

"*A raccoon?*" our mate on watch asked in disbelief.

Everyone quickly ran to the edge of the cargo hold hatch to see the damage. There he sat in complete isolation against the backdrop of the white salt: two gray streaks followed by two more black streaks. The loader didn't even flinch; he just slewed the loading boom inboard to get out of the way assuming that we were going down there to pull him out.

"*Well, it looks like he's a goner. That was kind of a long drop, and who knows what happened to him on the way here either,*" somebody said.

"*We should probably get him out. I mean, I doubt the customer wants a dead raccoon in the middle of his salt pile. It's kind of gross,*" said our deckhand.

Everyone continued to stare and come up with some new suggestions since this was not a usual situation. In the end, Craig, feeling sorry for the raccoon, agreed to go down into the cargo hold and dig him out.

We shifted the boat down the dock to put the loader in another hatch. This way Craig wouldn't have to worry about anything falling on him, or getting salt dumped on top of him.

With all eyes on him, Craig managed to get down the hardened steel ladder welded to the cargo hold side. A large jump into the salt pile and a climb over the peak would leave him at the foot of the recently deceased. We watched Craig climb up the enormous pile. With each movement of his leg, we could see his feet sinking deeper into the pile. Walking through eighteen thousand tons of salt is like walking through quicksand. The worst part is no matter what you do, your boots fill with the white chunks.

The plan was to lower a bucket down on a piece of rope, flop his little raccoon body in, and hoist him out. That was the plan anyhow until the little bugger was touched by the hand of God and reanimated himself right there in front of us. Not only was he far from dead but he was so alive he ran up the side of the cargo hold and into a tiny little space for protection.

Everybody was shocked! Craig looked up at us in disbelief. Then he quickly righted himself to figure out what was next. After catching his breath, Craig followed him up the tank side. He poked his head around and found him lying in the wire chase of the semi-darkness.

The rest of the crew, topside, encouraged Craig to come up. The novelty of the chase had worn off, knowing it would be nearly impossible to catch a raccoon in the cargo hold of a freighter. The circle of employees began to disperse. This would certainly be the end of a funny sea story. That is until they heard a terrifying scream reverberate through the cold steel chamber of the cargo hold.

"AHHHHHHH!"

Everyone turned to look but didn't see Craig at first. He eventually stumbled into view sliding down the steep tank side, clutching his hand against his chest.

Somebody said, "Oh my God, did he just do what I think?"

"Did he just get bit?" I heard someone else ask.

Craig looked up with his sad little puppy eyes. Armed with nothing but good intentions—not even a pair of gloves, mind you—he said, "But he just looked so cute. I couldn't help myself."

Hours later, he returned to the ship from the hospital.

The captain was shaking his head saying, "In all my years sailing, that's the first time I've ever had to send somebody to the hospital for a rabies vaccine."

Craig went back to work with some shots and stitches and the raccoon got a free ride to Erie, Pennsylvania, to start his life anew.

THE OLD AND THE NEW

The original car ferries on the Great Lakes were exclusively for carrying railcars. They did carry passengers, but automobiles did not ride until around the mid-1920s. There is a great old photo at the end of this chapter, showing a steam locomotive loading the car ferry *City of Midland*.

Some readers may also be railroad buffs. Because Mike was able to find the following details, we are including them here:

The Pere Marquette used 0-6-0 steam switch engines made by Alco for the car ferries. All these steam switch engines were off the Pere Marquette locomotive roster by 1948, and that was the last year that the coaling tower in Ludington was operational. The last steam locomotives C&O and the ex-Pere Marquette companies used were stricken from the rosters by 1954.

Pere Marquette R.R. started buying diesel switch engines in 1939: the SW1, Road #10. In 1942, they purchased another SW1, Road #11. In 1942 and 1943, they purchased four EMD NW2s, Roads #51 to #54. In 1945 and 1946 they took delivery of ten more NW2s, Roads #55 through #64. They also purchased a smaller quantity of diesel switch engines from another manufacturer.

Before the C&O took control in 1948 the Pere Marquette had 16 EMD diesel switch engines plus the others, which didn't survive long on the roster. EMD NW2s proved to be the most reliable. Many of these survived into the Chessie System–era.

On the current Lake Michigan car ferry, the *Badger,* cargo is still carried, but no longer in train cars. The ferry is popular with heavy and oversize semi haulers, to avoid the need for permits and other expenses going through Indiana and Chicago to reach Wisconsin from Michigan, or vice versa. See the photo at the end of this chapter.

CAR FERRY DANGERS

Car ferries presented some unusual dangers, due to the train cars carried as cargo. The following story from Mike Braybrook is both scary and funny:

Years ago, there was a "heavy weather" captain on the car ferry the Badger, *who would go out in almost any kind of foul weather. One mid-November day, we had come into Ludington ahead of a freshening wind out of the west and tied up in number two slip. While the switch engine was unloading the boat, we got news that the train coming into Ludington with our load had been delayed out east and wouldn't be coming into town till the following morning.*

That was good news for the crew because it meant anyone off watch could go home for the night if they were local. If they didn't live nearby, they could maybe catch a movie or hit the bar scene, and not have to worry about being back to the boat in two hours, which was the usual schedule.

The wind had been picking up all night, and by morning heavy waves were coming over the break walls. Once the boat had been loaded and the crew was all aboard, the captain decided he was going to sail out of the harbor, "stick our nose" into the lake to see how bad it was. I had the 4–8 watch and had been up since 3:15 a.m., so I decided to turn in and get some sleep. Kopey, the fireman on the same watch, had the room right across from mine and was also heading to his bunk. In the winter, anytime the boat was going to be in rough seas, the car handlers had to put up jacks and chains on all the railcars to keep them from rocking.

Normally the captain wouldn't leave the slip until all the cars had been secured, but that day, for some odd reason, he decided to go before they were finished. The lone car that hadn't yet been secured was on the outboard rail, just opposite the sliding door that went down to the flickers. The only two vehicles aboard for that trip—a pickup and a Pontiac Bonneville—were between the railcar and the flicker door.

As the boat went through the break walls it started to pitch and I could feel the vibration of the waves hitting the bow. About a mile out into the lake, the captain decided the seas were worse than he expected so he hauled the boat around to get back into the safe refuge of the harbor. As she started to come around, we got into the trough and began to roll heavily. I could hear the railcars above, creaking and groaning against their restraints.

Of course, there was that one railcar the car handlers had not yet secured, and it began to tilt back and forth on the rails. With one wild roll of the boat, the railcar swung against the ship's side, bounced back in the opposite direction, and fell completely over on its side, crushing the two vehicles next to it.

Down in the flicker, we heard a horrendous crash overhead, which caused me to jump out of my bunk to see what the hell happened! Across the hall, Kopey had also jumped out of bed, and in a flash, Kopey was in his doorway wearing just a T-shirt and BVDs, with his eyes wide open!

I quickly pulled on some pants and shoes, bounded up the stairs, and slid the door to the car deck open. Directly outside the door was the top of the bulk railcar. It was so close to the flicker door one couldn't get past it. The first thing I noticed was the smell of gasoline, as the tanks on both vehicles had been ruptured, and the gas was leaking out on the deck. At the same time, I could hear a muffled car horn blowing beneath the wreckage, likely because it had shorted out. Those two things were not a good combination.

So, I quickly slid the flicker door closed, and enlisted the help of Kopey and a couple of other guys to pull out some fire hoses, just in case. The boat had stopped rolling and started pitching instead, as the seas were now coming from astern, while we headed back towards the harbor. After we were tied up back in the slip, the crew and the office people from ashore swarmed around the toppled railcar, assessing the damage.

The sorriest parts of the story? The people who owned the pickup truck were moving to Nebraska and had some antiques in the back, which they didn't trust with the movers. The Pontiac Bonneville was brand new with only four hundred miles on it! See that terrible photo at the end of this chapter.

For the crew to get out of the flicker for their watch, or to go home, we had to use the emergency escape hatch, which opened farther forward, up through the car deck.

The bulk railcar was carrying granulated Peladow—ice melt, or calcium chloride—which had to be shoveled out by hand into wheelbarrows. That took two days. Then a specialized crane on a lowboy railcar had to be brought in to lift the car and get it off the boat. Meanwhile, the crew had a couple of days that they could spend at home when off watch, which was a welcome treat.

SPECIAL DUTIES

All commercial ships have drills to perform as required by the U.S. Coast Guard. The drills must be performed monthly and logs kept to document that they were performed. On cargo ships, the Coast Guard witnesses these drills once per year, and on the Great Lakes, this is usually done during the spring fit-out. The boiler alarms and steam pressure relief valves are tested, boat drills are demonstrated, and life jackets are inspected.

On passenger vessels, like the ferries, the Coast Guard observes some drills every three months to ensure passenger safety. There is a photo at the end of this chapter showing a crew from the *Badger* performing a lifeboat drill, and another showing Mike Braybrook, all dressed up in his life jacket.

Here is another great story from Mike:

Back in the late 1970s, I picked up a job on the Grand Trunk Railroad's S.S City of Milwaukee to help fit her out. She was tied up at the Grand Trunk lay-up dock in Muskegon, Michigan. The Ann Arbor Railroad in Frankfort needed to lease her to replace the Viking, which was a carferry that needed to go to the shipyard for dry-docking. After we had her all fitted out, and the steam was up on the boilers, the deck crew from the Viking came down from Frankfort on a bus.

Because her engine crew stayed with the Viking in the yard, a relief crew was gathered from the union halls and sent to Muskegon. Since all of them were new to the plant on the City of Milwaukee, they required some breaking in training, so Jim, the second engineer, and me as fireman stayed from the fit-out crew to train the new guys. Jim was to work with the engineers and oilers for the engine room, and I was assigned as a wiper—at a fireman's pay—to familiarize the firemen with the ship.

While the new guys were learning the job, I had to be in the boiler room during each watch when the boat was going in or out of port. I also had to be there when the boiler's burners were being changed, which was on every watch. The proper way to light off a furnace was to insert the torch, open the fuel oil valve, and count to three. If the fire didn't catch by then, the torch was to be pulled out immediately, the oil valve shut off, and the furnace purged before trying it again.

Well, one fireman was a little slow on the draw. I counted to three while watching him light a burner. He hadn't started pulling the torch out yet and just as I was about to yell, "Pull it out!" there was a loud bang as the accumulated vapors in the furnace ignited! The flue cap above his head, which weighed over four hundred pounds, blew off the boiler. It swung up, and, lucky for him, it lodged in some piping.

Soot and smoke from the fire tubes blew out in a big cloud, enveloping the fireman. His cap blew off his head and flew out of the smoke. For a split second, I thought it was his head! As he stepped out of the cloud of smoke, his face was all black, and I don't think I've ever seen a bigger pair of wide-open eyes! Except for the soot temporarily tattooed into his wrist, and in the gap between his sleeves and gloves, he was none the worse for wear.

However, much to his chagrin, his nickname for the rest of his time on the boat was Boom-Boom! Just before this all happened, the relief fireman had come down to take the next watch, and he was leaning on a stanchion. After it happened, I looked back at him, and he was still leaning against the stanchion. He was muttering, "Nope, nope, I ain't firin' this boat no more!"

Happily, for the rest of the month sailing for the Ann Arbor there were no more incidents … Well, except maybe for that one at Pea-Soups tavern in Elberta, but that's another story.

This job was expected to last the duration of the lease to the Ann Arbor Railroad. My room was in the flicker, where the engine crew lived, just aft of the engine room. The room was the nearest one to the watertight door into the engine room and was only about five steps away. Therefore, this was the shortest commute to work I've ever had in my life!

This was a different time on the Lakes when drinking aboard ships was the norm. It was technically not allowed, but those rules were regularly ignored. There happened to be a sign in the flicker that said, No alcoholic beverages allowed aboard this vessel. *Just below that was a smaller sign that said,* 'Don't throw trash or empty beer cans in #4 hold'. *(Resigning themselves to the inevitable?)*

The wiper is the engine room janitor and answers to the first engineer. First thing in the morning when I came to work, I would walk into the tool room. There I would always find the first engineer sitting near the coffeepot, and he would always toss me a cold can of Pabst beer to start the day, even before coffee! It was pretty much an order so what was a guy to do?

We were on a steady run between Frankfort, Michigan, and Kewaunee, Wisconsin. We had an oiler who was from Green Bay, and he kept his AMC Gremlin parked on the dock at Kewaunee, so he was the designated "beer truck." When the boys were getting low on libations, he would take orders and run up to the store. It was comical to see him come back with the rear of that Gremlin loaded down to the axle with cases of beer. As soon as the railcars were unloaded, he would back the Gremlin up the car deck to the flicker door, and several guys from the engine crew would be waiting to form a bucket brigade to get it all down below before the train came back with the return load. That was an enjoyable job and a fun crew. Too bad it only lasted a month.

In the next stories, Bill Kulka talks about explosions in shipboard boilers and other unusual events. It is never dull on a ship!

On the S.T. Crapo *(aka STC), once in a while there'd be an unexploded blasting cap in the coal (left over from the mines). That would wake up the firemen! We'd also burn trash in the STC's boilers. Once in a while, some asshole would throw a used spray can, which would explode. That would also wake up the firemen!*

More than once, usually due to weather, we'd be out in the STC's bunkers shoveling the corners to the screw conveyors. We'd come back to Alpena with just hours of coal left. In the fall, on a Lake Superior trip, we'd overfill the bunker, out onto the deck and up to the windjammers, just in case. The deck department hated that because they did all the on-deck shoveling.

While a young, dumb, second engineer on the Crapo, *I was inside a lit-off boiler in the other firebox, peening over some leaking rivets. I had the induced draft fan running for air and* was standing on 2x12 planks that were charring on the bottom from the heat. I'd wear a mask, goggles, gloves, and a wet wool sweater. The fireman would be outside with a hose, spraying me and/or the wood as needed. I look back at that and wonder what the #@%& I was thinking. Inside a sixty-five-year-old fire-tube boiler with old rivets and 180 psi on the other side?

The STC's three Manitowoc fire-tube boilers had geyser blow valves. The same valve could do both surface and bottom blows, depending on how you turned the big handwheel.

I wasn't aboard when this happened, but someone told me they did an underway blow and accidentally shut off one of the gauge glass valves instead of the blow valve. On that boat, the boilers held so much water and the level changed so slowly that both the engineer and the oiler watched the water level. They assumed the other watchstander had made adjustments and the level wasn't changing, due to the closed valve. The boiler's fuse plug did its job. the water slowly dropped, and the fuse plug melted. It snuffed out the fire in the boiler. There's a lot of water that flashes when that happens! They thought the boiler blew up. They said it sounded like a jet plane in the fire aisle.

On the Crapo, we also had a high-pressure cylinder cross-head pin bearing overheat. We made it to Alpena and took it apart to re-scrape. We were using a twelve-pound sledgehammer, taking turns banging on it. After my turn, I passed the hammer to a younger, muscular oiler. On his second or third swing, the hammerhead broke off, bounced off the engine, and coldcocked me. I do remember opening my eyes, on the deck, with the fuzzy face of the chief engineer over me! I had a lump on my head for weeks—maybe brain damage?—which may explain a few things!

Due to several bent passenger car bumpers, the Badger decided to remove a pair of bits from the car deck. We didn't use them, even at lay-up. When Bay Ship cut the first one off, there was an old empty bottle of Kessler that had been welded *inside it back in 1953. We had also removed some lockers and welded inside one base we found another empty Kessler bottle. Chief Cart returned them to the Bay Ship superintendent while at the yard. We also found a wrench, welded into the fire main piping, between two 90-degree bends, where it had also been since 1953.*

There are some good photos at the end of this chapter, showing the carferry Badger in dry dock.

The carferry *Badger* has been mentioned a lot during this section on car ferries. There is another photo at the end of the chapter—another postcard from my collection—showing the *Spartan*, which was a sister ship of the *Badger*.

The *Badger* was eventually raised to allow more automobiles to be carried on a "tween deck," which is a partial deck above the main car deck. Except for that change, they were built to be identical.

It is interesting to see the description on the back of this postcard:

> The S.S. *Spartan* and its sister ship, the S.S. *Badger,* are the new twin queens of the Great Lakes. They are the largest and finest ships of their type in the world. Pacing the Chesapeake and Ohio Railway's year-round Lake Michigan fleet of seven vessels, the train-ferrying steamers provide frequent service for passengers, autos, and freight between Ludington, Michigan, and Wisconsin ports of Milwaukee, Manitowoc, and Kewaunee.

Those were the good old days!

1. Typical Emergency Generator.

2. Full load of Harleys on the way to attend 100th anniversary.

3. Harley Davidson cycles boarding Badger, headed to Wisconsin.

4. Old steam engine loading rail cars on ferry at Ludington.

5. Modern semi-load of oversize cargo, loading on the Badger.

6. Two cars crushed when rail car tipped over in bad weather.

7. Lifeboat drill to satisfy Coast Guard regulations.

8. Mike Braybrook in life jacket.

9. Bow of Carferry Badger in dry dock.

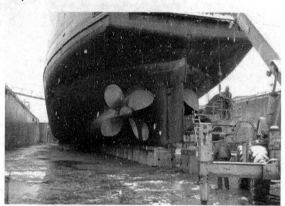

10. Stern of Carferry Badger in drydock.

11. Carferry Spartan, sister vessel of the Badger.

CHAPTER 11

Passenger Boats

There is one segment of Great Lakes shipping that is nearly forgotten: the passenger liners. These were the main mode of transportation for immigrants coming to the United States back in the nineteenth century. In this case, we are not talking about car ferries, which happen to carry passengers across Lake Michigan. These passenger liners typically operated between Buffalo, Cleveland, and Detroit on the east, to Duluth, Chicago, or Milwaukee on the west. There were other ports served, but these were the main ones.

Two of the pictures at the end of this chapter are from my postcard collection. The card showing the *City of Detroit* is postmarked November 1913. The man writing the postcard was in Detroit, trying to find a job at Ford Motor Company. He said thousands were waiting in line, so he was giving up, and would head to Buffalo to look for work.

Some of these ships had staterooms, but many of the immigrant families slept on benches and chairs. When the traffic of immigrant passengers slowed down, and the railroads began to have faster, direct service, the remaining passenger liners began making short family excursion trips from the larger cities such as Chicago and Milwaukee to vacation spots in Michigan and Wisconsin.

Another photo at the end of the chapter is the *City of Cleveland*, which is a sister ship to the *City of Detroit*. The back of the postcard describes the vessel, which carried 1,451 passengers and had 390 staterooms and a dining room that seated 225. They had a crew of 225, as well. You may notice the designation on the bow, *U.S. Mail*, which was common for many of these steamers. They were paid by the United States Postal Service to carry mail between the ports they serviced.

There were even day trips from Chicago to the beaches in Indiana, and some readers may be aware of the *Eastland* disaster in Chicago. On July 24, 1915, the ship rolled over onto her side while tied to a dock in the Chicago River. A total of 844 passengers and crew were killed, in what remains the largest single loss of life from a shipwreck on the Great Lakes. This led to much more stringent stability regulations for ships in general, but particularly passenger ships. The ship was built in 1903.

One of the more famous day trip excursion boats sailed out of Milwaukee, Wisconsin, the *Christopher Columbus*. It carried passengers to the Chicago World's Columbian Exposition in 1893. You will notice the strange hull shape; it was known as a "pig boat" due to the blunt nose. It is the only whaleback steamer to be used as a passenger boat. The others were only used to carry cargoes of coal or ore, or as tankers.

Most of these ships were laid up as tourists began taking weekend auto trips instead of boat trips, but one of the last to operate was the *Milwaukee Clipper* (or the *Clipper*). She was built as the S.S. *Juniata* in 1904, and carried 350 passengers in staterooms, in addition to those on deck. She has a riveted steel hull and originally had a magnificent wooden superstructure. When originally operated by the Pennsylvania Railroad, she carried passengers and freight between Buffalo, New York, and Duluth, Minnesota, with stops in between, until 1915. She was then operated by the Great Lakes Transit Corporation until 1937.

In 1939, the old cabins and wooden superstructure were removed and replaced with steel, to meet the new maritime fire safety standards.

The *Clipper* continued to operate on Lake Michigan until 1970 when the *Aquarama* was supposed to replace the *Clipper*; however, the *Aquarama* was too deep for Milwaukee Harbor, and that plan eventually fell through. But the *Clipper* has escaped the scrapper's torch, and it is now a beloved museum ship based in Muskegon, Michigan.

There are several photos of the *Clipper* at the end of this chapter from old postcards showing the her varying paint jobs over the years. One of the postcards notes some interesting facts about the ship:

New Luxury Liner of the Great Lakes. Twentieth Century Streamlining. Ultra-modern interior appointments. New designed air-conditioned cabins. Sun and Fun Decks for various shipboard games. Grand Ballroom. Unique Dining Buffet. Excellent Cuisine supervised by Master Chef. Smart Entertainment. Clean: Oil Burner. Capacity for 900 passengers.·

I was very involved with the *Clipper*, starting in 1974 when it was laid up at Navy Pier in Chicago. It moved back to Muskegon for a short period, where they made repairs to hopefully return her to service, and I surveyed the Clipper in Muskegon for that purpose. When that project fell through, she was sold to the port of Hammond, Indiana, as an attraction vessel. It was used for meetings and served some light meals. In May 1989, the ship was designated a National Historic Landmark. She was eventually displaced by a large floating casino—money seems to trump nostalgia—and then the S.S. *Milwaukee Clipper* Preservation Inc. organization, which now gives the *Clipper* the love and care she deserves, permanently moored her in Muskegon, Michigan.

You will see a photo of the *Clipper* being towed as it left Hammond harbor, if you look in the tugboat chapter of this book. More details of the *Milwaukee Clipper* can be found in numerous articles on the internet.

While researching the information for this story on the *Clipper*, I was lucky enough to contact Captain Bob Priefer, the last captain of the *Milwaukee Clipper*. Bob was ninety-six-and-a-half years old, per his daughter, at the time of this writing, though he said ninety-eight, and his memory was so sharp and detailed, it was amazing—other than when it came to his true age.

Bob worked for a short time in the food service segment of the *Clipper* when he was a young man. He then started sailing on tugboats, delivering Army tugs from Duluth, Minnesota, to the West Coast, and even sailed convoy duty to Europe during World War II. Bob not only sailed on the *Clipper* when he was on the Great Lakes but he told me he sailed ore boats in 1941 and sailed on most of the car ferry fleets. He also delivered a tanker, the *Gemini*, from Texas to the Great Lakes for Cleveland Tanker Company. But Captain Bob will always be remembered as the captain of the *Milwaukee Clipper*.

Captain Bob loved his job, and he said he seldom took much time off during the passenger season, which ran from Memorial Day until Labor Day. However, the *Clipper* did not lay idle during the fall and spring months, or even during winter, when ice conditions allowed. The *Clipper* was also a car carrier, and she carried newly built automobiles from Muskegon to Milwaukee. Those cars were then loaded onto railcars for transport to the western states. Both the *Clipper* and the *Highway 16*, a converted World War II LST (landing craft), were used in that Lake Michigan auto transport service.

The *Highway 16* now looks much better after conversion back to her original camouflage LST paint job.

Captain Bob told me about a couple of unusual events worth mentioning here.

Edmund Fitzgerald, then chairman of the Northwestern Mutual Life Insurance Company, was riding the *Clipper* one trip when it was going into Manitowoc. This is the Edmund Fitzgerald for whom the S.S *Edmund Fitzgerald* was named. Northwestern Mutual owned the ship. Captain Bob was asked to give Fitzgerald the "cook's tour" of the *Clipper* as they were entering Manitowoc. Manitowoc Shipbuilding was just finishing a new ship for Interlake Shipping. Bob stated that the new ship was one of the more beautiful ships he'd seen. He then realized Interlake was a major competitor of Fitzgerald's company, Columbia Transportation. Bob said he felt like he'd stuck his foot in his mouth.

I asked if they ever had trouble with rowdy passengers, like what sometimes happens on the Caribbean cruise ships. Bob said that was seldom a problem. When some became a bit boisterous, he'd go down and cajole them about putting them in the brig if they caused trouble. He laughed with them and the problem disappeared. Knowing Captain Bob's personality, his hands-on treatment of these things probably worked well. The passengers all knew who he was, and they respected him. It was not his authority, as much as his great personality, that prevented such problems.

Bob did say that some weekends when motorcycle fans came to Milwaukee for bike racing, they did have a lot of drinking on the *Clipper* and the crowd got a little loud. The following day, the same biker fans returned to Michigan, where the motorcycle hill climbing races occurred. Those weekends were sometimes a bit rowdier, Bob said, but never a huge problem.

While on the subject of car carriers, I was stationed on the U.S.C.G.C *Bramble* in Detroit 1964–65, and there were these two old car carriers, the *George H. Ingalls* and the *T.J. McCarthy*, which were moored just upriver from us. They had not run during the whole time I was there, and I later found they had been used to haul new-built automobiles from the Detroit factories to various ports around the Great Lakes. I'm sure some of our boat-nerd readers will know more details about them.

PASSENGER BOAT CREWS

Because the old passenger liners operated between two or three ports much of the time, the crews could get home on some sort of regular schedule, similar to the car ferries. Captain Priefer said his wife was a schoolteacher and they remained married throughout his career and beyond. His wife could visit the *Clipper* when it was in Muskegon, and some of the other crew members probably took advantage of their regular visits to their home port, unlike the crews on the Lake freighters. The *Clipper* sailed with 115 crew members, but only thirty-six of those were considered marine crew, covering the navigation, engineering, and ship maintenance jobs. The remaining crew was for passenger services, including the galley, customer service, entertainment, and other passenger related services.

1. Passenger liner, City of Detroit.

2. Sister passenger liner, City of Cleveland.

3. Passenger liner, Eastland.

4. Eastland disaster in Chicago River.

5. Whaleback passenger excursion vessel, Christopher Columbus.

191

6. Passenger liner, Juniata, became the Milwaukee Clipper.

7. Passenger excursion vessel, Aquarama.

8. Old version of the Milwaukee Clipper.

9. Newer version of the Milwaukee Clipper.

10. Car Carrier, Highway-16, converted LST.

11. Highway-16, returned to her original LST 393.

12. Two old Detroit car carriers after lay-up.

CHAPTER 12

Tugboats and Tugboaters

This book started by saying that Great Lakes sailors are different from deep-sea sailors, which is certainly true. However, there is a subset of Great Lakes sailors that is very different from the others, and these are the tugboaters. They may be close to the type seen in East and West Coast harbor tug operations, but on the Great Lakes, many of the small tug operators work on an as-needed basis. Some tugs sit at the dock for long periods, not operating at all, usually with no crew aboard.

The larger tug operators on blue water have cargo barge runs to Alaska, Puerto Rico, Hawaii, and so on. They operate much like the deep-sea cargo ships, but as a tug and barge combination, saving money on the crew size required. On the Gulf Coast, numerous large companies service the oil rigs, acting as anchor handlers and supply boats, and even towing the drill rigs from one location to another.

The large harbors, like New York, Philadelphia, San Francisco, and a few others, have small tug operators similar to those described on the Great Lakes, but nearly every major Great Lakes port has these operators, including Duluth-Superior, the Soo—Sault Ste. Marie—Detroit, Toledo, Buffalo, Sturgeon Bay, Escanaba, Milwaukee, and Chicago. Other tug operations are part of marine construction and dredging companies as well. Looking at *Greenwood's Guide to Great Lakes Shipping*, there are over twenty-five companies that fit this description, and that is ignoring those dedicated, articulated tug-barge units, which are closer to ore carriers. This also ignores the large number of Canadian-flagged tugboats.

In my previous books, I mentioned an old black-and-white movie series starring a lady called Tugboat Annie. She was a fictional character but was located in New York Harbor. She was a boisterous woman, with a larger-than-life personality. At the time, I figured she was just a great character, but how could a woman act that tough? Some of the female tug operators on the Great Lakes either took lessons from Tugboat Annie, or they did have similar personalities. I think it takes a strong personality to compete in the tug business and many of their employees come from a tough breed, so the owners need to be strong to get the necessary cooperation from their crews.

The Great Lakes has many of these small tug operators, and although each is different in their operating details, they are very similar in most respects. I will first highlight the Great Lakes Towing Company, which is the largest on the Great Lakes. Their history goes back to 1899. They had been affiliated with, but not part of, Great Lakes Dredge and Dock Company. The Great Lakes Towing Company has two or more tugs in twelve ports around the Great Lakes. Over the years, they also had operations in Florida, Puerto Rico, and Hawaii, and leased some of their ocean tugs to other tug companies. The Great Lakes Towing Company has unionized employees, but the crews are not generally full time, although most are guaranteed a minimum number of hours per pay period. Other than supervision and maintenance personnel, they are on call, as needed, which will be described further in the next paragraph. Because of less business in smaller ports, crews are shuttled between some of them, like Duluth, Green Bay, and Milwaukee.

The "on call, as needed" way of operating the smaller towing companies is what makes them very different. The ore boats and car ferries have both licensed officers and crew under contract unless there is a layoff. Those Laker crew members had a job on some sort of schedule, whether it was "stay until we tell you to go home," which was true up until the 1970s, or you worked sixty days on, thirty days off once those union contracts started. The car ferries had a "twenty days on, eight days off" schedule.

The small company tugboat owners call the crew when they have work, though. They might have kept a few key people on standby status—with some lesser pay—performing maintenance, but the average crew member was called to come to work whenever the tug company got a job. As you can imagine, the small tug operators could not afford to pay people to just sit and wait for something to happen.

The amazing thing is those crew members normally did come to work when they were called. Many of them might have had a hangover, but they came to work. Whether it was family loyalty, the loyalty of the local townspeople to the owner, decent pay when they did work, or just the desire to do tough—and sometimes exciting,—work, often under dangerous and miserable conditions, they usually showed up. Many of them did not have a higher education, and they had no other marketable skills. Some hated the idea of humdrum, day-after-day work in a manufacturing job, such as in the shipyards. A forty-hour week was just not appealing to them.

For this reason, the tug owners always found men willing to work on the tugs, despite hot summer tows, terribly cold winters of ice breaking, and the danger. This is not as true today, and since around the year 2000 willing crew members are getting harder to find.

Part of the attraction may have been their friends' admiration for these tugboat sailors, and sailors in general. Tugboaters probably had a few drinks bought for them, as they related their crazy, and exciting, escapades from their last towing job. Although the circumstances are quite different, service during the Vietnam War was once described to me as 98 percent boredom and 2 percent pure terror! Those who could deal with the 2 percent went back for more. Maybe this is how some tug crew members feel.

The Great Lakes tugs typically perform the following work:

- Assist towing of large vessels entering harbors and into shipyards
- Assist towing during shipyard side launching (only at one shipyard)
- Ice breaking in rivers, harbors, and shipyards
- Towing cargo, lashed to large deck barges
- Towing dead-ship vessels (non-powered) on long, cross-lake tows
- Emergency towing, due to ship accidents, groundings, etc.
- Moving small barges from rivers to local lake ports, generally Chicago to Burns Harbor, Indiana, or Chicago to Milwaukee
- Moving oil, asphalt, cement, and other small barge cargoes

Tugboats have relatively small crews, and the owners tend to invoice by the hour, which covers the cost of the crew, fuel, and other expenses. Plus, they need to make enough money to pay their bank loans, as the tugs need to be bought and eventually be replaced.

Some jobs, such as dead-ship towing and the barge towing of cargo, are bid against other tug operators, so there is a proposed price to do a specific job. These can be lucrative, but also have the most risk, because weather delays, ice conditions, and other unforeseen conditions must be considered in their bids.

ASSIST TOWING

This type of towing is pretty much what it sounds like. The tugs, usually one on the bow and one on the stern, assist a larger vessel, usually when the larger vessel is in congested waters or has to navigate a channel with a lot of bends in the river. The tugs may also assist the vessel to dock at its pier by pushing it close to the dock, so the mooring lines can be placed on the bollards. This is important in windy weather, or if strong currents make it difficult for the ship.

Many newer vessels have bow thrusters, and some even have stern thrusters, so assist towing has been affected by the addition of thrusters. In some ports, the ships have no turning basin near their docking position, and the ship captains may prefer to enter the harbor stern first, so they will still request tug assistance for their stern-first entry. They then depart without tug assistance. In fact, some freighters even back into rivers alone, without assistance.

There is a photo at the end of this chapter, taken during an assist tow that I observed as part of an operational compliance survey.

Shipyards use a lot of tug assistance to move ships or barges around the shipyard during new construction, or during repairs of existing ships that have no crew aboard and the ship's engines are not being used. On the Great Lakes, because much of the non-emergency shipyard dry-docking occurs during the winter, tugs are also used to break the ice around the ships and the dry docks to enable the ship to enter the dry dock.

A special type of shipyard assist towing occurs when a newly con-structed ship is side launched at a shipyard. The ship slides sideways down the launching ramps and hits the water. Tugs are stationed near the launch site, and they quickly come up against the launched vessel and control its motion, so it cannot drift into the adjacent channel or into shallow areas.

Assist tugs generally have large-diameter propellers, providing high torque, as well as over-sized rudders to provide good maneuver-ability at slow speed. Pushing power is developed by larger diameter propellers turning at slower revolutions per minute (or rpm). Small-diameter propellers can develop similar horsepower, but not the torque, turning at higher rpm. This is not effective at the slow speeds required to move a much larger vessel.

Randy Wilke relayed this story from his experience when Selvick Marine Towing was acting as an assist tug for a new ship headed out on a restricted river for its first sea trial:

This was our first assist tow for the LCS shipbuilding pro-gram in Marinette, Wisconsin. We were hired to assist the first LCS built at Marinette Marine to safely exit and enter the harbor for its sea trials. The contract required that we attend a meeting and dinner on Sunday night, with the U.S. Navy and Marinette Marine personnel, to discuss and plan the next morning's events.

On Monday morning, we started our tug up at 0400 and sailed over to the LCS. We made our three-inch nylon harbor line fast to the bow, and we waited for the 0600 departure time.

We departed right on time and we only had to give a light tug on the bow to get her off the dock. The rest of our assist was to be with a slack towline, so they could demonstrate how maneuverable this new class of ship would be.

Everything was going as planned for the first mile into our 1.5-mile tow, heading out to Green Bay, but then we came up to the only bridge we had to go through. The bridge was closed to vehicle traffic to give access to the large number of news media crews. They wanted to film the ship leaving on its first sea trials.

We were just starting to enter the bridge draw with our tug, with the ship right behind us, lined up in the center of the draw. All of a sudden, the bow of the ship dropped quickly to starboard. The ship was now going to hit the right draw of the bridge!

Our tug captain saw this, and received a frantic call from the ship. I also started yelling to our captain over the deck PA system, telling him to pull full to port. We realigned the ship in the draw, and they narrowly cleared the bridge. The rest of our tow went fine.

It just goes to show, you never know what can quickly go wrong when working on a tug. And the best part was, the news media never knew how close that first LCS came to a very embarrassing damage on her first sea trial.

ICE BREAKING

As mentioned previously, ice breaking is used in and around ship-yards. Tugs are also used during the fall and spring months to break ice in harbors when the freighters are ending their seasons, or just starting the season. The Coast Guard cannot be in every harbor so tugs are used unless the ice conditions are so bad that the Coast Guard must be called. This saves the ship's valuable time that might be lost waiting for Coast Guard assistance to arrive.

The tugs lead the freighters out of the harbor and out to open water. This also saves some of the wear and tear on the freighter's hull, which occurs when moving through solid ice.

CARGO TOWING

Tugs are often used to tow barges that are loaded with cargo and lashed for safe transit. Shipyards occasionally have sub-assembled modules built at other facilities, which are then moved by barge to the shipyard for final assembly.

Other manufactured products such as large industrial boilers are moved from the manufacturing facility to the end destination by loading the equipment on barges and then towing the barges with a tug.

Another photo at the end of this chapter shows the loading of equipment on a deck barge in Sarnia, Ontario. The equipment was transported to Chicago, where it was then loaded into several river hopper barges, to be transported to a factory in Alabama.

A common problem occurs when large equipment is imported, but there is not a customs-approved port facility near the final destination. The imported cargo must be unloaded at a customs-approved port of entry and loaded onto a barge once it has cleared customs. The cargo, like large diesel engines, as shown in another photo at the end of this chapter, can then be transported to the final destination with a tug.

DEAD-SHIP TOWS

This is similar to assist towing, except these tows are usually longer in distance, and the towed vessel's propulsion machinery is not operational. This can occur when an old vessel is being towed to a scrap yard, or, as described in the car ferry towing story, when a vessel is being towed to a shipyard for repairs, such as those who are familiar with the *City of Midland 41*, which was towed to another destination for modifications.

The big difference between assist and dead-ship tows, is that for a longer dead ship tow, the client will typically ask several towing companies to provide a cost proposal before making a decision. For assist towing, either a long-term contract exists between the towing company and client, or a quick cost is requested for an hourly or daily charge for the assist.

There is a photo showing a dead ship tow of the *Milwaukee Clipper*, at the end of this chapter, when it was leaving Hammond, Indiana. It eventually ended up in Muskegon, Michigan, as an attraction vessel.

The following story is about an unusual dead-ship tow of two newly constructed barges, for which I was hired to do a towing approval:

> In September 2000, I was hired by a large marine insurance underwriter to survey two large Navy barracks barges. They were being towed from the Great Lakes through the St. Lawrence Seaway. One was headed to Norfolk, Virginia, and the other was headed for San Diego, California.
>
> The barges were not built for ocean service and would be permanently moored to the dock at the two Navy shipyards. The ship's crew stayed aboard these barges while their ship was in dry dock and it had sleeping and galley services for a large number of sailors.
>
> My services were meant to ensure the barges would survive the towing voyage relative to weather, although I also placed weather restrictions on the tugs to seek shelter in bad weather. The bows of the barges were lightly built and my concern was the heavy chain towing bridle that was laying across the deck. Normal sea motion would cause the chain to wear through the headlog plate (bow plating), which was only 3/8 of an inch thick. Despite the shipyard's and tugboat owner's complaints

about the delay, I convinced the underwriter that a thick doubler plate needed to be installed over the headlog, where the chain would rub.

The tow went well, with several delays due to weather. One barge went to Norfolk and the other continued through the Panama Canal to the shipyard in San Diego. There is an article in Volume 56 of Inland Seas: Quarterly Journal of the Great Lakes Historical Society *that describes the voyage. Multiple Great Lakes tugs were used (five in all) to safely pass all the restricted narrow waterways, including two from Selvick Marine and two from Gaelic Towing.*

Several years later, while attending a condition survey of a World War II–built special Navy vessel in Norfolk, I saw that the barracks barge occupied the same dry dock as the vessel in for inspection. I looked up at the bow and saw that my doubler plates were still installed. I related the story to my Navy guide that day, and he said it was a good thing I had convinced the shipyard because the chain had nearly worn through the doubler.

EMERGENCY TOWS

When an accident occurs and one or more ships are disabled, or if a ship runs aground, a towboat is usually needed to assist. If the vessel is in immediate danger, the tug will tow the vessel to a place of safety; however, because an insurance claim will be made, it may be necessary to get approvals from the damaged vessel's insurance company. The insurance company may designate a marine surveyor to make decisions on their behalf. This process is meant to reduce the expenses as much as possible, which will eventually become part of the claim.

Some tugs carry some limited salvage equipment to be used in these instances, such as portable pumps and oil-retention booms to confine any oil spills, and they can obtain other supplies from shore as needed.

In the chapter on unusual events, one of Mike Braybrook's stories described the failed emergency generator that required a tug to bring them back to Manitowoc to discharge passengers, and then tow the disabled car ferry to Ludington for repairs. This was a good example of an emergency tow.

SMALL BARGE MOVES

Although this is an everyday occurrence in Chicago because of the large number of barges that come up the Illinois Waterway, there are other similar moves, which will also be explained.

There are numerous river hopper barges and small tank barges that move through Chicago, generally from Calumet Harbor. They often carry steel from the Indiana steel mills, as well as other dry bulk cargoes, which are allowed to be moved in fair weather across the lower end of Lake Michigan. The Coast Guard has also approved similar moves to Milwaukee and several ports on the west shore of Michigan. Tugs generally based in Chicago, move these barges to and from those ports very regularly, sometimes daily.

There are also oil refineries in Indiana shipping products, generally asphalt from the Chicago area refineries, that eventually head down the Illinois Waterway in small river-sized tank barges.

Some of these moves are made by river towboats—square-bowed pusher tugs—but the small Great Lakes tugs are more efficient for these moves, and they make most of them.

CROSS-LAKE COMMODITY TOWING

Although some of these commodities are the same as the small barge moves described above, particularly the oil and asphalt, these tend to be larger barges that carry a load line. This means these barges can legally transit the entire Great Lakes, not just those restricted Chicago routes, in fair weather only.

The tugs used for this service are larger. Some are considered tug-barge units, with the tug securely fastened in a notch in the stern of the barge. These larger units typically carry cement and oil products.

In addition to those commodities, this type of towing also includes marine construction materials, like large break wall stone, rubble stone, and other aggregates, for the Army Corps of Engineers harbor projects. In some cases, the Army Corps of Engineers will contract with the tug operator to supply the stone, or the tugboat will be operated by a marine construction contractor carrying stone for a project they are performing, either for the Army Corps or a private party.

One of the more unusual barge tows is shown in another photo at the end of this chapter. I represented the underwriters for the Great Lakes Towing Company during the operation, removing an old bridge span, which was then scrapped.

Towing jobs do not always go as planned, however. I surveyed a damaged tugboat and the damaged crane that the tug was towing between two lower Lake Michigan ports. It was a short tow and the weather was good, so the tow across the lake went fine. This same tow had been accomplished just a few weeks before, so the tug operator saw no need to request assistance from a Marine surveyor, and he left the crane boom raised, just like the previous tow.

Upon entering the river, the crane, which was securely mounted on the barge, needed to move under a railroad bridge, which had been raised for the tug and barge. The one thing the tug operator's foreman had failed to notice was that this crane had one more section of boom installed. This made it taller than the crane on the previous tow. See the photo at the end of this chapter, which shows the result. Note the crane boom is supposed to be pointing in the opposite direction. The tug captain, not the foreman, barely escaped the pilothouse before the roof was crushed when the boom fell backward.

Another unusual towing job came about when a research vessel in Muskegon, Michigan, sank. I was hired to oversee the salvage of the sunken vessel and then to properly secure it on a barge so it could be towed across Lake Michigan to Bay Shipbuilding. The intention was to repair the vessel but that never happened. Two photos are included at the end of the chapter, showing the vessel being raised by a crane, and then loaded on a barge.

TOWING CAN BE DANGEROUS

Randy Wilke shared the following story that happened while he was working for Selvick Marine Towing:

In late 2000, we were in Manitowoc, Wisconsin, making an assist tow for a three-hundred-foot-long barge. The barge and tug were from Canada and the Canadian tug captain did not want to take the barge through the bridges on his own. They were heading to a dock upriver to load two large stainless-steel tanks.

Our tug, the William C. Selvick, *was at the bow of the barge on the bridle towline, to guide the bow through the bridges. The tug* Steven Selvick *was faced up to the barge, guiding the stern. The Canadian tug was following us in to offload a crew at the dock. The crew would moor the barge when we got there.*

The tow through the bridges and the turnaround of the barge went just fine. As we completed the turnaround and were approaching the dock, we noticed the Canadian tug was still there. The captain on my tug radioed the Canadian telling him to move because we were approaching with the barge. My deckhand and I were standing about mid-tug watching the action.

As the Canadian tug started to quickly back away, we noticed their tug might collide with our bow so the deckhand and I quickly moved to the stern. The Canadian did strike our bow fender, tearing four feet of the fender free. The force of the collision spun our tug sideways, and our towline put us under the bow rake of the barge. Because of forward momentum, the rake of the barge was now sinking our tug by riding over us. We already had twelve inches of water over the main deck at the stern and up to midships.

I grabbed our fire ax to part the towline, hoping that would free us. Before I struck the towline, I noticed the water starting to come off the main deck so I didn't part the line. One of our deckhands up on the barge calling distances for our other tug saw what was happening, and told our stern tug to back full. That stopped the momentum, allowing our tug to right itself. We were able to get back onto our towline, so we could complete the tow. This just goes to show you always need to be on guard when working on a tug.

There is a picture at the end of the chapter showing the short towline used when making an assist tow, or in this case moving an unpowered vessel during a shipyard assist tow. Because of these short towlines, the vessel can easily overtake the tug when things go wrong.

TUGBOATER'S JOBS

Some of the roles and duties of tugboat crew members include the following:

- Each tug has a licensed captain, at least when operating outside the harbor
- Most tugs have an engineer, but they are not required to be licensed on the Great Lakes
- One or two deckhands typically sail
- Other men, like a welder and welder's helper, may sail on cargo tows, but they are normally obtained locally, and not carried aboard

These tugs run very lean on personnel compared to the large crews on ore boats and car ferries. The tug companies' best way to stay competitive on contracts is to keep the number of crew members to a minimum. This tendency to keep the crew to a minimum also creates a danger of working alone in the dark, with heavy seas and on icy decks. There are many stories about losing men over the side on the Great Lakes, both on tugs and cargo ships.

Until recently, there were no serious regulations for tugboats. The safety, crewing, and conditions of their hulls and machinery were unregulated. To prevent the Coast Guard from over-regulating the industry, the American Waterways Operators (AWO) instituted a voluntary audit program that was endorsed by many of the major oil refineries and other manufacturers shipping their products by barge. If the tugs wanted to move these cargoes, they had to become an AWO member, pass the AWO audit process, and be an AWO-approved towing company. I was an AWO Responsible Carrier Program auditor for twelve years during that period.

This AWO program worked for a while, but the Coast Guard finally prevailed, and Subchapter M of the Coast Guard Code of Federal Regulations now requires all towing vessels twenty-six feet in length or longer to carry a Coast Guard Certificate of Inspection (COI). This will increase safety among the tug operators but many of the smaller tugboats cannot meet these requirements without exceeding the value of the tug. Many will eventually be scrapped and some smaller companies are suffering serious financial problems to obtain Subchapter M certification for their aging fleets. There are a lot of new tugs being built twenty-five feet and 11.5 inches in length to skirt this new regulation.

The following is an interesting tugboat story from Mike Braybrook, which also involves a car ferry:

> When the car ferry City of Midland was scheduled for towing to Muskegon, to be cut down to a barge, Selvick [Marine] Towing was hired to do the job. Six of us—all car ferry crew members—were going to ride the tow, and two of the Lake Michigan car ferry owners were originally going to ride also. They decided at the last minute to ride the tug instead.
>
> After the tow was well out into the lake, the two owners were regretting their decision to ride the tug. Being on the tug wasn't exactly what they expected it to be. They found the smells alternating between diesel fuel and diesel exhaust. Then there was the constant engine noise to deal with, which they certainly weren't used to.
>
> When supper time came along, the engineer came up and went into the galley, where the two owners were sitting at the mess table. He casually wiped most of the oil off his hands with

a dirty rag and reached into the fridge. He grabbed a package of pork chops, opened it up, and pulled out a few chops using his fingers, and started throwing them on the grill top. At this point, he asked them if they wanted something to eat, which they politely declined.

On the tow, those of us on the ferry had brought sub sandwiches to eat, knowing we had no way of cooking anything. The chief was a bit upset with himself because he forgot to bring along some portable lighting to use after dark. We were going to need it while handling lines in Muskegon. All we had were flashlights, which we had parked on the mess room table. We had gathered there to B.S. while waiting to arrive at Muskegon. After some time had passed someone wisely suggested that we turn them off because the batteries weren't going to last forever. So we continued talking in the pitch black.

Once we finally came up against the dock in Muskegon, we had some help with lighting via the vehicles on the dock, which had turned their headlights on at our request.

There is a photo at the end of the chapter from a similar event, when a tug was preparing to tow the carferry *Badger* from Ludington over to the shipyard in Sturgeon Bay.

To show the size differences of the various tugs on the Great Lakes, I've included several photos at the end of the chapter. Most of the larger tugs built as part of an articulated tug-barge unit, have been built specifically to push one barge. The tug has a connection system that holds it in a large, deep notch in the stern of the barge. The tug is removed from the notch only for maintenance, like the following photograph shows. Otherwise, the tug is permanently secured in the notch, except for some emergencies.

There are a few tugs that have been converted to push barges in an articulated mode. Some come from ocean service, and one such tug used the engine room from a Great Lakes freighter, which was removed and rebuilt into a tug.

One of the photos not only shows the tug but also shows the notch in the barge, where the tug is secured.

Many of the medium-sized tugs on the Great Lakes were originally built as ocean-going tugs. Many of them were Navy or Army tugs, which were obtained at government surplus auctions.

The smaller Great Lakes tugs were either built for Marine construction companies or were harbor tugs from the East Coast or Gulf of Mexico ports. Many of them were built to tow oil field equipment, and each time the oil business slumps, those tugs become available for other towing operators.

SPARE TIME ACTIVITIES

Tugboaters are not normally known for great leisure time activities, mainly because they work when there is work and go home when there is no work. However, Mike Braybrook knew a guy named Russ who sailed tugboats as well as Lake freighters and carferries. Here is a short story and an example of Russ's artistic skill:

> Over the years I've sailed with several fellas that sailed on Lakers, car ferries, and tugs. One was an AB, by the name of Russ, who sailed on a tug for a while, then took a relief job on a thousand-footer. That was quite a culture shock. After that, he picked up a steady job on the car ferry out of Ludington, so he sailed on all three types of vessels in a relatively short period.
>
> There is a copy of a sketch at the end of the chapter, which Russ drew in the mess room on the tug, where he was working for those years.

THE OLD AND THE NEW

As mentioned above, many of the tugboats on the Great Lakes have been purchased at auction from the U.S. Army or the U.S. Navy, and in recent years, many of the tugs built for the ocean oil drilling trade have been purchased by Great Lakes tugboat companies, whenever there is a slowdown in the Gulf of Mexico oil business.

However, some tugs have been built specifically for the Great Lakes. One particular example are the "G-Tugs" built by the Great Lakes Towing Company (Great Lakes). Many of those G-Tugs—called this because of the large G on their stack—are still running, although they were originally built in the 1910–1930 time period. Great Lakes is now replacing the oldest G-Tugs with new tugs, specifically designed for the Great Lakes harbors.

Those old tugs were originally steam-powered, but Great Lakes bought many of the diesel engines sold by the U.S. government after World War II and repowered those tugs. Some of those tugs are now on their third set of propulsion, as well as new diesel generators.

Many of the marine construction companies also had similar situations, using repowered Army and Navy tugs for their cross-lake towing. The tug *John Purves* is now a museum in Sturgeon Bay, Wisconsin. It is a prime example of a large ocean tug, repurposed for use on the Great Lakes for salvage operations.

There are several photos at the end of this chapter, some showing the typical, older tugboat pilothouse, having the large steering wheel, where the tug operator stands and steers the vessel.

Other photos show a modern tugboat pilothouse where the pilot sits in a raised seat, with joysticks being used to control the vessel. This modern joystick system is not yet common on the Great Lakes, but it has become standard in coastal harbor tugs and in what are typically called tractor tugs.

The last photo in this chapter is taken at sunset in Sturgeon Bay, showing the tugboat fleet, taken by Randy Wilke.

1. The author, riding tug during an assist tow in Chicago.

2. Assist tow of LCS vessel in Menominee River.

3. Tugboat in ice, Sturgeon Bay, Wisconsin.

4. Tugs breaking ice in Sturgeon Bay Canal.

5. Cargo being loaded on barge for Great Lakes transit.

6. Large engine being loaded on barge for Great Lakes transit.

7. Dead-ship tow of Milwaukee Clipper from Hammond, IN.

8. Barge loaded with an old bridge in Cleveland, Ohio.

9. Crane damaged during tow, under a lower than expected bridge.

10. Research vessel Halcyon sinking in Muskegon.

11. Loading salvaged Halcyon on a barge for transit to shipyard.

12. Dangers of short-line assist towing.

13. Tugboat Jimmy L pushing the Carferry Badger.

14. Typical large Great Lakes tugboat.

15. Combination Tug/Barge unit, separated in drydock.

16. Typical medium-sized Great Lakes tugboat.

17. Typical small-sized Great Lakes tugboat.

18. Leisure-time crew member artist on a tugboat.

19. Typical old tugboat pilothouse

20. Typical new tugboat pilothouse.

21. Modern Great Lakes tugboat.

22. Sunset with Sturgeon Bay tugboat fleet.

CHAPTER 13

Great Lakes "Boat Nerds"

The term *nerd* may have a negative connotation in some uses, but a "boat nerd" is just a way to describe a "groupie" who follows ships and boats. To some of us in the industry who have come to just take ships, boats, and other related subjects for granted, we watch and listen to boat nerds and think of them as a bit weird, but yet wonderful to watch and listen to them. Boat nerds come to narrow points in the rivers and port entrances on the Great Lakes just to watch the vessels go by. They wave to the crew and they take pictures. They post those pictures on social media, and there are probably fifteen or more Facebook pages dedicated to various segments and aspects of the Great Lakes Merchant Marine industry. How many other groups of nerds have a webpage dedicated to them? See the last website listed in the On-line References list at the end of this chapter.

Some of the photos of Great Lakes freighters used in this book were used with the permission of very professional photographers, recommended by Captain Lori Reinhart. They probably started as simple boat nerds, but their artistic craft has led them well beyond that entry level into Great Lakes ships. They love Great Lakes shipping, and their photos display that. Although some of these photographers have been mentioned in the chapters above, I would like to credit them here:

Glenn Blaszkiewicz

Paul Scinocca

David Shauer

Terry White

Charlie Smith

Jeff Doty

Thank you, gentlemen!

One of our photographic contributors for this book, Ken Ottmann, is a great example of a boat nerd. As described previously, the term "boat nerd" is in no way derogatory. These people love ships and in particular Great Lakes ships. That love goes beyond the ships themselves and extends to many related subjects, and some, like Ken Ottmann, have developed lifelong friendships with other boat nerds. The following story, edited from Ken's own words, describes these ship-lovers better than any other I've seen:

I never worked on the ferries but have ridden them since the early 1950s. My mother never drove, and her Polish family had immigrated to Baltimore and settled in Manistee, Michigan. Before the turn of the last century, the job market in west Michigan was not as good as the market in Milwaukee, so my grandfather moved his family to Milwaukee. For my mother traveling to Michigan to visit family, the most direct and cost-effective method was via the car ferries.

On my father's side of the family, my grandmother was of Dutch heritage and she had grown up on the fringe of Jones Island on Stewart Street. My fraternal grandfather was a steam engineer for a Milwaukee construction company. He instilled in my dad a love of steam engines and steamships. My dad became a mechanical engineer, owned his tool and die business, was involved with race cars and airplanes, and had a fascination with ships. I'm seventy-two now, and Dad is long gone, but because of my dad, I developed a love for

Jones Island [in Milwaukee] and all that went on there. I still love auto racing and aviation, too, but love of the car ferries is probably the greater part of the transportation equation.

After college, I started hanging out on my own down at the car ferry dock on Jones Island. I got to know several crew members by just starting up conversations. At the same time, I met other boat buffs. Art Chavez and Tony Robles were the first guys I met. They were still in high school. Then, on a goodwill cruise for City Fathers, when Michigan-Wisconsin Transportation took over the operation, I met Doug Goodhue and John Hausmann. John was about ten years older than me, and he had documented all of the Lake Michigan car ferry operations from about 1970, with 8mm movie and 35mm slides.

The five of us became lifelong friends, though we lost John Hausmann a few years back. Art, Doug, Tony, and I rode the car ferries the Badger and the City of Midland regularly. We got to be known by the crew, and someone dubbed us the "Milwaukee Mafia." We were given carte blanche access to the boats, and many crew members became family for us. We were invited into the homes of several crew members, and I had several crew members stay at my house over the years.

Of our car ferry buff group, Art Chavez was the only one to have worked for a car ferry company. He was an auto attendant at Jones Island for the C&O for a couple of summers. Doug Goodhue went down to the Gulf and worked as a seaman on oil supply boats for a few years. He wrote for his five-hundred-ton captain's license and worked as a mate and then captain of a dinner cruise boat here in Milwaukee.

Sadly, life gets in the way of all good things. I got married and had a daughter, and years later Art and Tony also married. My wife and daughter love the Badger as much as I do. Art's daughter and mine are second-generation car ferry buffs.

They have a tradition of making a round trip on the Badger *on the last weekend of her operation each fall.*

I retired in April 2012 and was offered a position on the board of directors for the Society for the Preservation of the S.S. City of Milwaukee. The S.S. City of Milwaukee *is a retired railroad car ferry permanently moored in Manistee, Michigan. I went to Manistee to volunteer on the boat, just for the love of the boat, but I found a group of fellow volunteers who are great people. I keep hanging out there for the love of the people as much as for the love of the boat.*

As for my car ferry family, all of them have retired, several are in nursing homes, many have died, and a small handful remain friends. Captain Gregg Andersen and my family are the best of friends. Dan Bissell, a son of Captain John Bissell, remains in close contact.

Last but not least is retired junior engineer Mike Braybrook. Hardly a day goes by that Mike and I don't exchange messages via the great internet. Mike is one of the core volunteers at the City of Milwaukee. *The core volunteers gather monthly from spring through fall to keep our old gal in shipshape condition, as our limited budget will allow.*

There is a picture at the end of the chapter showing our two boat nerds, Mike Braybrook and Ken Ottmann, during one of their working weekends at the museum, carferry *City of Milwaukee*.

ONLINE REFERENCES

If the readers have caught the "boat nerd bug," the following social media, websites, and particularly Facebook pages, are recommended. Many of the Facebook groups require a request to become a member, but normally just expressing an interest in their subject matter is sufficient for approval. The following list is current as of the writing of this book but is only meant to be a start for those interested in learning more about Great Lakes maritime history. You will find many more links as you look through those in this list.

Helpful Facebook pages include the following:

- Great Lakes Shipping History
- Great Lakes Shipping Channel
- Great Lakes Ship Chasers
- Great Lakes Passenger Liners
- Fans of the *Milwaukee Clipper*
- Great Lakes Towing & Shipyard
- Wisconsin Marine Historical Society
- Great Lakes Marine Antique Collectors

The below are some other good Internet links to get you started, too:

- Minnesota Historical Society: collections.mnhs.org
- Chronology of Great Lakes Navigation: nmu.edu and search for Great Lakes
- Maritime History of the Great Lakes: Images. MaritimeHistoryOfTheGreatLakes.ca
- Great Lakes Shipwreck Museum: ShipwreckMuseum. com
- Great Lakes Lore Maritime Museum: gllmm.com (see their links)
- Michigan Maritime Museum: MichiganMaritimeMuseum.org
- Historical Collections of the Great Lakes: www.BGSU. edu and search for Great Lakes History
- www.wikipedia.org and search for Great Lakes

Boatnerd.com is almost a complete source of information on Great Lakes shipping and recommended books on Great Lakes-related subjects. So, once you have exhausted our list, be sure to go to boatnerd.com.

To show how serious a boat nerd can be, there are two photos at the end of the chapter showing a house on Lake Erie. The house is the actual forward deckhouse off the S.S. *Benson Ford*, now showing the name as Frank J. Sullivan, who is the man who bought it and moved it to that location. Sullivan wanted to use it as a hotel, but the current owners use it as a holiday home.

The *Benson Ford* hauled iron ore and coal for the Ford Motor Company. It was built in 1924 and was decommissioned in 1981. It was being scrapped. Frank Sullivan bought the deckhouse and moved it to this location.

The former ship's interior still contains the original wood-paneled staterooms, dining room, galley, and lounge designed by Henry Ford. Thomas Edison was a former frequent passenger on the *Benson Ford*.·

For those who wish to learn more about the life of the sailors, both Great Lakes and deep sea, there are some great books available to you. Read Captain Frank F. Farrar's book, *A Ship's Logbook*, for a good explanation of deep-sea sailing contracts during the same 1930–1970 sailing period, when Captain Farrar sailed deep sea. It is very interesting and well worth reading.

It was not the major effort of this book to look at each crew member's life in detail, but if you would like to learn more about these excursions "up the street," told by a deckhand who sailed on the Great Lakes, read *Lake Effect: A Deckhand's Journey on the Great Lakes Freighters*, authored by Richard Hill. Richard's descriptions of his life aboard ore boats over the late 1960s into the early 1980s are well told, in great detail. A second, similar book, *Deckhand: Life on Freighters of the Great Lakes*, authored by Nelson Haydamacker and Alan D. Millar, also tells great stories about their escapades ashore.

I suggest you read *Shipwrecked: Reflections of the Sole Survivor* by Dennis Hale, who was the lone survivor of the *Daniel J. Morrell* sinking. Not only is his description of the incident itself very dramatic, but his experience with survivor's guilt and his description of life aboard that ship, are very good. There are many books written about the sinking of the *Edmund Fitzgerald* but choose a factual one for the whole story. Many of the stories fail to properly deal with the later investigations and the true cause of the accident.

1. Two old Boatnerds, Mike Braybrook & Ken Ottmann.

2. Freighter Benson Ford bow.

3. Benson Ford bow used as residence in Lake Erie.

About The Author

Bob Ojala earned a BSE in Naval Architecture and Marine Engineering from the University of Michigan, Class of 1970. Bob also spent four years in the U.S. Coast Guard, seventeen years with the American Bureau of Shipping, and eight and a half years with the U.S. Army Corps of Engineers. Bob also worked thirty years in his own business (which does include the time while with the USACE). He is still active in marine surveying.

Bob is a Wisconsin native with Finnish roots, and his father was a merchant mariner for thirty-two years. This gave Bob an interest in the maritime industry, but not the desire to be a sailor.

Bob worked as a Naval Architect, designing small passenger vessels, tugs, and barges after graduation. However, he found he enjoyed working in the shipyard with the workers more than sitting in the design office.

When the opportunity came to join the American Bureau of Shipping, working as a field surveyor, inspecting ships and equipment going into shipbuilding, Bob thought this was what he was looking for!

Eventually, Bob started his own marine surveying and consulting business. Because Great Lakes clients were slow in changing loyalties, he traveled the world, surveying cruise ships, tankers, dry docks, and even some warships. He also investigated accidents, pollution incidents, and several accidental deaths.

Bob always wanted to document his father's career as a sailor on the Great Lakes but saw that it was important to document all of the Great Lakes sailors, not just one segment of the industry. This book tries to show the differences, and probably some similarities, between Great Lakes and deep-sea sailors, and also to describe the various segments of the Great Lakes: ore boats, car ferries, and tugboats.

With this background, Bob felt that he could describe the life of these merchant mariners and compare the Great Lakes versus the deep-sea sailors with some accuracy. If a reader disagrees with any of the details, please let Bob know; as he is not averse to revisions.

CPSIA information can be obtained
at www.ICGtesting.com
Printed in the USA
LVHW052340110321
681235LV00012B/1740